FOR
THE CITY
OF THE
VIOLET CROWN,
AND ALL
THE WEIRDOS
WHO CALL IT
HOME.

TABLE
oF
CONTENTS

INTRODUCTION 7

Boomtown Austin 8

The First Rule of Tex-Mex 9

Restaurant-Style Cooking 11

The Central Texas Pantry 12

CHAPTER/1

BARBECUE

Central Texas–Style Smoked Brisket 24

Smoked Sausage 27

From-Scratch Kielbasa 29

Smoked Turkey 31

Ribs 32

Smoked Pork Shoulder 35

Barbecue Sauce 37

Brisket Frito Pie 38

Chipotle Slaw 40

Jalapeño Cheese Grits 41

Traditional Pinto Beans 42

Jalapeño Dill Potato Salad 43

CHAPTER/2

TACOS

Braised Pig Tail Puffy Tacos 49

Basic Braised Pork for Tacos 51

Carne Asada Tacos 52

Old-School Carne Molida Tacos 55

Chicken Tinga 57

Tacos de Hongos 58

Banh Mi Tacos 61

Wild Boar Carnitas 63

CHAPTER/3

TEX-MEX and INTERIOR MEXICAN

Bob Armstrong Dip 70

Guacamole 75

Rice and Beans 76

Green Chile Queso 77

Chile con Carne Enchiladas 79

Chipotle Lamb Loin Chops 82

Chayote Slaw with Chile Arbol Dressing 84

Mole Rojo with Chicken 86

Enchiladas Tejanas 88

Butternut and Goat Cheese Chile Relleno 91

Cochinita Pibil 93

CHAPTER/4

TEXAS STANDARDS

Chicken Fried Steak with Cream Gravy 99

Pimento Cheese 100

Mustard and Brown Sugar–Crusted Ribeye 104

Pommes Puree 106

Grilled Tuscan Kale 107

Lucy's Fried Chicken 108

Parkside Macaroni 111

Blackened Drum with Shrimp Cream Sauce 114

Baked Oysters 117

Meatloaf 118

Okra with Walnuts 120

CHAPTER/5

NEW AUSTIN CLASSICS

Uchiviche 125

Beet Fries 127

The Cadillac Bar Pie 128

Oxtail Pappardelle with Rutabaga 130

Duck Confit with Lemon Vinaigrette Frisée and Duck Fat–Roasted Potatoes 132

Chorizo Potato Pizza 134

Sunshine Roll 137

Tom Kha Gai 138

Grilled Quail with Green Mole 141

Sauerkraut Johnnycakes 143

Bakra Goat Burger 144

Pig Skin Noodles with Shrimp Dumplings and Hot Sauce 147

Sweet Potato Nachos 151

CHAPTER/6

BREAKFAST and BRUNCH

Potato and Sausage Breakfast Tacos 159

24 Hash 160

Huevos Rancheros 167

Migas 168

Texas Benedict 169

Pumpkin Bread French Toast 171

Gingerbread Pancakes 172

Beef Tongue Empanadas 174

CHAPTER / 7

DRINKS

Mexican Martini 180

Frozen Margaritas 183

Fresh Lime Margaritas 185

Cucurbit 186

Horchata 188

Colorado Bulldog 188

Cactus Jack Cocktail 189

Mezcal Old Fashioned 189

Joanne Cocktail 191

Wundershowzen Smoothie 193

CHAPTER / 8

BAKED GOODS and SWEETS

Pumpkin Bread 197

Cheddar Biscuits 198

Bootsie's Buttermilk Pie 200

Everything Bagel Kolache 203

Pecan Pie 206

Salted Brown Butter and Dark Chocolate Pecan Cookies 209

Daniel Vaughn's Banana Pudding 211

Texas Citrus Scones 213

CHAPTER / 9

SALSAS, SAUCES, and CHILIS

Pico de Gallo 217

Vegan Lentil Chili 218

JAK's Salsa 221

Salsa de la Casa 222

Salsa Macha Verde 223

Grapefruit Salsa 225

Pickled Jalapeños 226

Hot Sauce 227

Chile con Carne Sauce 229

Verde Sauce 230

Ranchero Sauce 231

FURTHER READING
234

ACKNOWLEDGMENTS
235

INDEX
236

INTRODUCTION

Austin is hot a good nine months out of the year. Actually, hot is just the beginning: The last couple weeks of July, we move way past hot. And this is not a languid, lazy heat I'm talking about. It's stiff and aggressive. The air seizes up around you, and nightfall doesn't bring any relief. Harsh light fades street signs and peels paint off cars; the grass turns brown and crispy. Austin stays hot past Labor Day, past the first day of school, long after the rest of the country has cozied up to their sweater weather and pumpkin-spiced treats.

But people here live outdoors. The lines for barbecue can be just as long in April as they are in August, the bar patios just as full. *A little hot weather isn't going to stop us from enjoying this city,* and I don't believe it's that famous Texan stubbornness at play.

The food's just that good.

The barbecue in Austin needs no introduction: The smoked brisket, ribs, and sausage around here are world famous. And the tacos! Breakfast tacos, of course, but there's a taco for every meal here. And we do indeed know how to pour a decent margarita, whether you like yours top shelf or strawberry frozen.

Austin's food prowess doesn't stop there. We've always had food trucks (where do you think the tacos come from?), but in recent years there's been an entire food truck renaissance. We have more fine-dining restaurants than ever before, and a whole world of international restaurants have opened. *You can now get food in Austin you wouldn't have dreamed of a decade ago. And as for the barbecue and tacos and margaritas, they're still around. In fact, they're better than ever.*

The world has noticed. Austin's restaurants regularly receive national acclaim, and the city has become a destination for hungry travelers. On any given weekend, you'll find throngs of tourists not just here for the music scene or University of Texas football (hook 'em). They come for the barbecue and the tacos and the sushi and the mezcal and the food trucks as well.

Except in August. In August, we keep the city to ourselves. Who else would wait for barbecue in that heat?

Boomtown Austin

Ask anyone who has lived in Austin longer than about a year and they will sigh and tell you how the city has changed. Some of them will mourn the good ol' days, when the rent was cheap and the beer was cheaper. But one thing that's definitely better now than in the good ol' days? The food.

When I first moved here in 2006—that's right, I'm not from Texas—the Austin restaurant scene was just beginning to emerge from its hippie diner and Tex-Mex dive reputation. There were a few bright spots, of course, and Austin has always had great barbecue and tacos, but in many ways this was still a college town better known for its music scene than its food.

That was about to change. A food revolution was happening across the country, and Austin became one of its hubs. People move here from all over Texas and the rest of the country, bringing their food traditions and flavors with them. Locals and transplants alike turned the city into a buzzy home to food trucks and farm-to-table restaurants and, yes, *launched a revolution in American barbecue.*

Old Austin hasn't disappeared: The air still smells like wood smoke and the tortillas are still fresh. Kerbey Lane's still here, as are Magnolia Cafe and Matt's El Rancho and Maudie's and more. And while not everything has survived the city's boom—the much-beloved Las Manitas comes to mind—many institutions still carry the torch of old Austin. We can still find our beloved cheap beer and breakfast tacos; now we can turn around the next night and dine at some of the best restaurants in the country.

Austin became such a hotbed for restaurants because this city is blessed with unbelievable natural resources: the incredibly fertile food traditions of Central Texas, a nearly year-round growing season, and a seemingly endless supply of passionate young entrepreneurs. Pair these with *a hungry citizenship that has never met a patio it didn't love*—not to mention the festivals that bring sun-starved tourists to town every spring and fall—and you've got the ideal environment for a major restaurant city.

The First Rule of Tex-Mex

Here's how I learned to love Tex-Mex, and began to love Austin.

When I was twenty-two years old, I put my cat and everything I owned into a Honda Civic and drove straight down I-35 from my college town in Iowa, basically on a whim. I had never been to Texas before. The plan was to spend a year waitressing and drinking beer in Austin and then ship off to grad school. *Except I never left.*

I did get a job waitressing, though, at a Tex-Mex restaurant near my house. At first it was a disaster. The clientele couldn't understand my ridiculously thick midwestern accent, and I was so unfamiliar with the food that *I had to ask what migas were before my first brunch shift.*

But, eventually, I learned how to pepper my waitressing pitch with *y'all.* I learned the food and clientele well enough that I could almost predict what a table would order just by looking at them. This guy's going to try to impress his date by adding top-shelf floaters to their margaritas, the girls' night out table of twentysomethings are all ordering sour cream enchiladas and chicken fajitas, the older couple will have the same puffy taco combo platter they've been sharing each week for thirty years.

There was one woman in her seventies, Dorothy, who came in a couple times a week in the middle of the afternoon. She always ordered the same thing: *a single beef tamale with chile gravy and a Colorado Bulldog.*

A Colorado Bulldog is basically a White Russian with cola poured in it—it tastes better than it sounds. We served it in a tall, tulip-shaped glass, the kind that typically holds an old-fashioned ice cream sundae. The restaurant only had a couple of these glasses, and we kept them tucked away on the top shelf of the bar. (Why we didn't stash them somewhere easy in anticipation of Dorothy's arrival is beyond me.) It took long enough to retrieve the glass that the bartender on shift would keep an eye out for her car through the window during the after-lunch slump, and start making the drink before she even entered the restaurant.

The last week or so that I worked there, Dorothy came in and I told her I was leaving for a new job. She smiled and asked me if I knew why she ordered that lone tamale every time. Turns out her late husband used to come in with her every week and get the full order: three tamales, smothered with chili gravy, with rice and beans on the side. He'd eat two and the rice and beans; Dorothy would eat one of them.

I asked her what the deal was with the Colorado Bulldog. "Honey," she said, *"you sleep in the same bed with a man who eats that many tamales, you're gonna need a stiff drink."*

That's the day I learned the first rule of Tex-Mex: Always get exactly what you want. Don't order the margarita just because everyone else in the restaurant is ordering margaritas, get the drink you truly want, the one that comes in the glass that's a pain for the bartender to reach. Order the single, off-menu tamale as a memorial to your late husband; eat only half if you're not hungry. *One of the beauties of Tex-Mex is that it's an endlessly customizable* cuisine—that's why they make the combo platters, after all—so if you're not getting *exactly* what you want, you're doing it wrong.

That's the beauty of Austin, too. *This is a different city for every single person who has ever loved it.* If you want old Austin, those places still exist. If you want new Austin, there are endless options to explore.

The Austin I love is a mix of both old and new. Here, you'll find Tex-Mex next to food trucks, diner breakfast next to fine pastries. My goal for this book was to include a little bit of everyone's Austin, whether you were born and raised here, went to the University of Texas for four years, or came here once for SXSW. If you don't see your favorite restaurant, know that it simply means Austin is too jam-packed with amazing restaurants to fit them all in one book.

No matter what your Austin looks like, I sincerely hope you see it in these pages.

Restaurant-Style Cooking

The dishes in this cookbook come from some of the great Austin restaurants. In fact, in many ways this book doubles as a restaurant guide. The recipes were selected to highlight what's unique, beloved, and/or especially Texan about each place, and they will help you re-create a taste of Austin in your own kitchen.

These recipes have not been dumbed down or simplified from the restaurant versions. While many of the recipes are easy enough for beginners, this isn't really intended to be a book full of quick weeknight meals. Every single dish here has been tested in my home kitchen, and I promise they are all possible in yours—given enough time, a little bit of skill, and the right equipment. (To be clear, I'm not talking mad-scientist-futuristic-million-dollar food lab stuff here, I'm talking offset smokers and pizza stones.)

Often, these dishes have more components than a typical home-cooked meal, with sauces and garnishes galore. In fact, many of the garnishes are great on their own, like the corn nuts on Odd Duck's Sweet Potato Nachos (page 151), or the Grapefruit Salsa (page 225) for the Swift's Attic puffy tacos (page 49).

There are also recipes that use very specific ingredients, especially when it comes to spices, seasonings, booze, and other flavorings. I urge you to use these ingredients where you can in order to get your dish as close to the restaurant's version as possible. In other words, you can use whatever type of bottom-shelf swill tequila you like in your margaritas, but it will only taste like Fonda San Miguel's if you use a 100% agave silver tequila.

Some of these dishes are super traditional, while others take modern liberties. **This might not be how your grandmother makes chile con carne** (or kolache, or macaroni and cheese, or pecan pie), but rather how each restaurant envisions the dish. Austin's restaurants pride themselves on their tasty creativity, and that's what is highlighted here. Accordingly, some of these recipes will seem more intensely seasoned than what you're used to, or maybe a bit fussy. Know that every step and ingredient is included to help you achieve restaurant-quality results.

The Central Texas Pantry

Austin and the surrounding regions are blessed with multiple growing seasons and access to regionally beloved ingredients, such as fresh flour tortillas, local grapefruit, a wide variety of fresh and dried chiles, and multiple styles of "party cheese" (Velveeta being the most common nationwide). Here's a quick guide to using common regional ingredients, with substitutions listed where it's appropriate.

BLACK PEPPER: More than any other flavor, *Central Texas tastes like black pepper.* It flavors Texas-style barbecue, plays prominently in Tex-Mex, and is used in everything from cocktails to breakfast dishes. It may seem like kind of a basic spice to form the backbone of a regional cuisine, but when you use it in the quantity Texans do, it becomes pretty distinctive. This is not a time to fuss with a pepper mill—some of these recipes call for up to ¼ cup (28 g) of pepper. In these cases, the preground stuff is suitable. Stock up.

BLACKENING SEASONING: Blackening seasoning is a spice blend typically associated with Cajun cooking, but it occasionally pops up in Texan food as well. Several recipes in this book call for blackening spice, and instructions are provided for blending your own (page 115). (Leftovers of which will keep in an airtight container in the pantry for months.) However, store-bought blackening spice is a totally acceptable shortcut.

CHAYOTE: Also called mirliton, chayote is a vegetable related to squash, cucumbers, and melons, and it is often used in Latin American cooking. If you can't find it, you can substitute any summer squash, but chayote has a unique texture that's worth seeking out.

CHEESE: First of all, you must use processed cheese where it is called for. *Get out of here with your cheese snobbery.* The recipes that call for processed cheese will not work with any other kind, so don't even try.

The most common brand of processed cheese is Velveeta, but any variety will do. American cheese is slightly different from processed cheese, although you can use them in recipes more or less interchangeably. (The texture will be slightly different.) If you cannot find blocks of American cheese in the cooler at your grocery store (you don't want to use the plastic-wrapped, presliced stuff), ask at the deli meats counter.

Recipes that require a yellow, melty cheese typically call for mild cheddar, but Colby would also work.

As for Mexican cheese, this book makes use of three: Oaxacan, Cotija, and queso fresco. If you can't find Oaxacan cheese, you can substitute Monterey Jack. The textures of the other two cheeses are a bit harder to replicate, but a mild, crumbly feta would work in a pinch.

FRESH CHILES: The spiciness of a fresh chile will vary depending on the season. Removing the seeds and veins will tone down the heat, but even *the relatively mild jalapeño can light a fire if it's in the mood for it.*

CHILE POWDER: Many different varieties of dried chile powders and blends are available, from chipotle to pasilla to ancho to Sneaky Pete's 17-Alarm Texas Chili Seasoning. (I made that last one up, but specialty blends abound.) Try to use the variety called for, but in a pinch you can swap it out for whatever you can get your hands on—even if it's just a generic jar labeled "chili powder."

CHILE SALT: Chile salt blends are more common in Mexico than in the United States, but they're incredibly popular in Texas. Brands like Tajín are delicious sprinkled on freshly cut fruit or used to rim drinks like margaritas or the Cucurbit (page 186).

CHIPOTLE: Chipotles are smoked jalapeños. You can get them canned in a tangy vinegar-based adobo sauce, as dried whole chiles, or ground into a powder. Recipes throughout this book call for all three varieties.

CHORIZO: Mexican chorizo is a spiced bulk ground sausage. (There's also a Spanish chorizo, but that's entirely different from what we're talking about here.) Buy the highest quality you can find because, first of all, it tastes better, and second of all, some low-end varieties contain fillers.

CREMA: Crema is similar to sour cream, except it doesn't separate when heated. If a recipe calls for crema, don't try to substitute sour cream—crème frâiche or even heavy cream would be a better substitute.

CUMIN: Cumin is another prevalent spice in Texan cooking—a cook I interviewed for this book referred to it as "Tex-Mex pepper." You can buy ground cumin, but if you want full impact, buy the whole seeds, then toast them and grind them yourself.

GRANULATED GARLIC POWDER: Over the course of writing this book, it became very clear that if a dish had a secret ingredient, it was either going to be soy sauce or granulated garlic powder. Granulated garlic powder is a very specific ingredient: It is not simple garlic powder, or garlic salt, or roasted garlic powder. It has a different texture and flavor. I'm not saying these dishes won't be good if you substitute one of these inferior garlic powders for granulated garlic powder, I'm just saying they won't be correct.

GRAPEFRUIT: We're lucky enough in Texas to have access to local citrus. Texas grapefruits often have juicy, red interiors—Ruby Red grapefruits first appeared here—and can be kind of, well, ugly on the outside. Don't let that deter you: The fruit itself is tart and bright and much more flavorful than standard grocery store citrus.

MASA: Masa is made from ground, nixtamalized corn—the same process used to create the corn nuts on page 153. Masa is what goes into corn tortillas and corn chips, as well as puffy taco shells (page 49) and masa empanadas (page 174).

PAPRIKA: Paprika is another spice that's prevalent in Texas cooking, likely due to the influence of nineteenth-century Czech immigrants. It's often used for its brick-red color as much as its flavor. There are several types of paprika out there; generally speaking, mild paprika will work best in these recipes.

PECANS: *Pecans are everywhere in Austin. Everywhere.* My house has five pecan trees on the lot, and starting in October it thunders pecans on the roof every time it gets windy. Thankfully, there are all kinds of ways to put this natural bounty to work.

If you don't live in Texas, use the highest quality pecans you can. They'll be expensive, but it's worth it for good pecans. If you do live in Texas (or Louisiana, or Arkansas, or Oklahoma, or . . .), make friends with someone who lives with a pecan tree and get cracking. Have you heard how much your northern friends are paying for nuts that are literally falling from the sky for free? Don't be ungrateful.

PEPITAS: Pepitas are the dried hulled seeds of pumpkins. You can buy them raw and toast them and salt them yourself, or buy them preroasted. These are mostly used as garnishes that add a vital crunch and earthy flavor.

PRICKLY PEARS: Prickly pears are the fruit of the nopal cactus. You can also find them in stores under their Spanish name, *tunas*. Prickly pears are most often a deep, delightful pink, making anything made from their juice unmistakable. They're called "prickly" for a reason—this is a cactus we're talking about—and they need to be carefully peeled before consuming. It's easiest to stick a fork in the fruit's end to hold it steady, then use a sharp knife to cut off the outermost layer.

SEAFOOD: Gulf seafood is recommended for all the seafood recipes in this book. Austin is a few hours' drive from the Gulf of Mexico, and eating fresh seafood here is not as outrageous as our landlocked status might lead you to believe. It was not that long ago that the future of the Gulf and its seafood was uncertain, thanks to the horrific damage done by the Deepwater Horizon oil spill. Thankfully, good-quality shrimp, oysters, and fish are still available from the Texas coast. So eat them.

TEQUILA/MEZCAL: Always 100 percent agave, but beyond that, use what you like.

TORTILLAS: Walk into almost any Austin supermarket and you're going to see a pile of freshly made corn and flour tortillas, steaming up the plastic bags they're sold in. I understand that good tortillas can be hard to find, especially flour tortillas. No matter what you have access to, get the freshest tortillas you can and make sure you heat them before serving (see page 48).

WILD BOAR: Wild boar is an invasive species to Texas, and they cause crop destruction, property damage, and car accidents all across the state—see Chef Jesse Griffiths's explanation on page 64. Thankfully, they're also delicious. You can order wild boar online, or, if you live in Austin, you can purchase it at the Dai Due butcher counter. Otherwise, substitute pork.

CHAPTER 1

BARBECUE

Where There's Smoke, There's Barbecue

The smell of smoke curls up from every corner of Austin, whether it's coming from a neighbor's backyard or the barbecue trailer down the street. It's a thin blue smoke, typically created by smoldering oak logs, and its scent is a hallmark of Austin just as much as live music, bats, and the University of Texas Longhorns. It wouldn't be entirely out of the question to FOLLOW YOUR NOSE to amazing barbecue in this city.

For a long time, the most famous barbecue in Texas was just outside of Austin proper. Renowned restaurants like Louie Mueller Barbecue in Taylor, City Market in Luling, and the famed Lockhart trio of Kreuz Market, Black's Barbecue, and Smitty's Market are all an easy drive from Austin.

But in 2009, everything changed. Aaron Franklin's story is now the stuff of barbecue legend: Charming guy from Bryan, Texas, in square hipster glasses opens a barbecue trailer by the side of the freeway. Fueled by dozens of shots of espresso and the best post oak Central Texas has to offer, he made some maddeningly good barbecue.

Franklin Barbecue indeed proved to be just the beginning. It was now abundantly clear not only that Austinites wanted to eat high-quality craft barbecue, but that smoked meat fanatics were willing to fly into town and wait in long lines for the privilege. And in the years that followed, pitmasters got to work: Stiles Switch BBQ & Brew opened in 2011; La Barbecue and Micklethwait Craft Meats opened in 2012; Kerlin BBQ opened in 2013. And that's just a small sampling. The result? Today Austin is a destination for barbecue fans from around the world.

The Trinity

As for what's smoking? The holy trinity of TEXAS BAR-BECUE: brisket, ribs, and hot guts sausage, all three dressed up in little more than salt, pepper, and smoke.

Brisket is the most famous of these, a notoriously tricky cut of meat to smoke properly. But when you hit that sweet spot, when the fat renders properly and a bark sets up on the outside, when the tough meat finally gives in to hours and hours of low, smoky heat, it is the very FINEST thing to eat in the entire Lone Star State.

Ribs are either pork or beef. Pork ribs are cooked until tender but not falling-off-the-bone, lending themselves gorgeously to a light salt-and-pepper rub. Beef ribs are the gonzo option of Texas barbecue: I'm not joking when I say they are often the size of a small cat. Believe me when I say you'll be fine with one to share.

HOT GUTS SAUSAGE is my personal favorite. Here, *hot* means spicy and *guts* means natural casings—Texans aren't ones to mince words. They're typically made with coarse-ground beef (sometimes mixed with pork) and the very best versions snap when you bite into them. When cooked, they're often loaded with spicy red grease, so roll up your sleeves and grab some extra napkins.

Texas barbecue isn't limited to these. You'll also see pork shoulder; pork steaks; Czech, German, and Polish sausage; chicken; turkey (do not sleep on the turkey—sometimes it's the best thing on the menu!); mutton; and even more creative options like smoked beets.

On the side, you've got old-school sliced white sandwich bread—often Texas brand Mrs. Baird's, rarely but deliciously homemade—that is doled out by the half loaf. You've got onions and pickles, which you shouldn't skip, as they're your allies in cutting the rich fat of the meat. There will be sauce, either peppery and thin or thick and sweet, and its use is a controversial but personal decision everyone must make for him- or herself.

There are sides from coleslaw to potato salad, beans to mac 'n' cheese. There might also be sandwiches loaded with chopped beef (brisket mixed with sauce) or sliced sausage, and baked potatoes piled high with the same. Beer is often BYO, although more and more Austin barbecue joints serve local brews such as Live Oak or Austin Beerworks. And for dessert, of course, there's pie and banana pudding (see chapter 8).

Hope you saved room.

A Crash Course in Smoking Meat

THE SMOKER

It all starts with the smoker. The least frustrating way to develop your barbecue skills is to use the highest-quality offset smoker you can afford. But it will cost you more than those cheap, shiny black smokers you see parked outside the supermarket. Potentially a lot more.

The cheaper the pit, the thinner the metal, and the more the temperature will fluctuate over the course of your cook. "If you have a thin-walled pit," explains Bill Kerlin of Kerlin BBQ, "it's going to be constant frustration trying to keep the temperatures consistent." The thicker the metal on your pit, the more it will cost, but the better it will hold a consistent temperature—perhaps the trickiest barbecue skill to master. In other words, you get what you pay for.

These recipes were tested on a mid-level store-bought metal offset smoker. I didn't mess with my pit in any way, although a quick internet search will lead you to all kinds of modifications you can make to improve smokers. You can also use these recipes with a vertical or ceramic kamado smoker. Whatever you use, follow the manufacturer's instructions for using your pit.

THE FUEL

Central Texas barbecue is most often smoked with oak, although hickory and pecan are also used (mesquite is common in South and West Texas, too). Traditionally you'd smoke with an all-wood fire, but I've found that using a mixture of charcoal and wood (chunks/small logs of wood, not chips) can help even out the temperature and make things easier on beginners. When you're just starting out, use charcoal to manage the temperature and use wood for flavor.

LEARN FROM YOUR MISTAKES

I'm not going to sugarcoat this: Learning to smoke barbecue can be a frustrating process. Briskets will take longer to smoke than you want; ribs will dry out; you will run out of charcoal before the cook is done; your thermometer will break; your guests will drink too much beer before food is served. Don't despair. The only way to learn how to smoke barbecue properly and reliably is to keep practicing.

- A chimney starter.

- A long grill lighter.

- Aluminum pans and heavy-duty aluminum foil.

- A good thermometer, ideally digital, for the meat.

- A good thermometer, ideally digital, to measure the temperature of the smoking chamber.

- A long (12-inch/30.5-cm) slicing knife.

- An empty can (a 28-ounce/794-g tomato can works well) to put under the smoker to catch grease. Your smoker probably has a hole drilled in the bottom where the grease drips out; the empty can goes under this.

- Some means of moving the meat around: long tongs or rubber-coated gloves. (Lance Kirkpatrick of Stiles Switch recommends buying thermal gloves at a restaurant supply store, and then slipping disposable food service gloves over them. "We do everything by touch," he says, "and that way you can just grab the brisket.")

- Closed-toe shoes. Do not—do not—smoke meat in flip-flops.

IGNITION

Prepare coals in a chimney starter according to instructions. Dump the lit coals in the firebox portion of the offset smoker. Nestle a couple logs in the coals to get the smoke started. Shut the door of the firebox, then open the firebox vent and the lid of the smokestack slightly.

You should start to see billowy white smoke come out of the smokestack. You do not want to cook with this smoke, or your meat will taste ashy and bitter. Wait for it to subside; in its place you'll soon start to see the famous thin blueish smoke rise out of the stack. This is the GOOD STUFF.

Generally I recommend waiting to put your meat on the smoker until you've maintained the required temperature for about half an hour. This way you know you've got it stabilized for a little while, and that bitter white smoke will have burned off.

HUMIDITY

Keep the interior of the smoker humid. Put a small empty can or disposable foil pan filled with water in the smoker next to the firebox, and replenish the water as it evaporates during the smoke. This will do all kinds of helpful things during the smoking process, from helping to maintain an even temperature to getting you over the dreaded cooking stall (more on that later).

MEAT POSITION

Lance Kirkpatrick, of Stiles Switch, explains that "Central Texas–style barbecue is fat side up, and you never flip it over." Typically you want to place the thickest part of the meat closest to the firebox, with the fatty side up. You also want to take the internal temperature in the thickest part of the meat.

FANNING THE FLAME

The trickiest part to smoking meat—the biggest hurdle to overcome—is learning how to maintain a consistent temperature. Mastering this skill is the difference between jiggly, glistening, wondrous barbecue and terrible dried-out chunks of meat cardboard.

The ultimate goal is to keep the temperature within about a 10-degree window of the recipe's recommended temperature, all the while keeping an eye out for that good, thin blue smoke. Got a lot of what Kirkpatrick calls "smoky white smoke"? He says that means "you're suffocating your fire and you need to let it breathe more. That's a big mistake a lot of rookies make." Time to crack those vents.

Otherwise, if the temp starts going down, add charcoal a little bit at a time until the temp starts going back up. Add wood when you need more smoke. You'll get a feel for it as you go. And remember, "More smoke is NOT always better," says Kirkpatrick. "Less smoke is usually better."

TIMING

Most of the recipes call for you to smoke the meat until it reaches a specific internal temperature. Some recipes estimate how long this will take, but if you're a beginner smoker, everything will likely take longer than you think it will, because you're not yet skilled in maintaining that necessary even temperature.

So plan ahead, and start early. Daniel Vaughn, of *Texas Monthly*, advises, "If you think your brisket's going to take twelve hours to cook, well, don't start it twelve hours before you want to serve it. Start it sixteen, seventeen hours before you want to serve it." Part of this is because the meat will need to rest (see opposite), but it's always best to budget extra time.

THE STALL

When you're smoking larger cuts of meat—brisket, pork shoulder—there will come a time when progress will seem to halt entirely. The temperature of the meat will be going up at a good clip, and then, boom: the dreaded stall hits and suddenly you're stuck at the same temperature. For a while. Maybe hours. There are scientific reasons for this—for more, check out the books mentioned in the barbecue library on page 30—but mostly it's just a huge pain.

Purists will keep on trucking at this point, smoking through the stall, but to speed things up a bit, you can wrap the meat in traditional butcher paper, or parchment, or foil. (Individual recipes will recommend different wrapping material.) This will get you through the stall in time for dinner.

THE IMPORTANCE OF RESTING MEAT

The larger the cut of meat you're smoking, the more important it is to let it rest. A brisket will need to rest until its internal temperature reaches 140 or 150°F (60 or 66°C), or as long as three hours, which is how long Kirkpatrick rests the briskets at Stiles Switch. Pork shoulder, as Bill Kerlin makes it, only needs about half an hour.

Vaughn explains why resting is important: "If you cut into it early, all that collagen that you worked so hard to break down into gelatin is super hot and still liquid. It will just flow right out onto the cutting board and you're never going to get it back." Don't let that happen!

You can rest barbecue wrapped in butcher paper on the counter for an hour or so. If you really want to get serious about things, rest meat in a Cambro or a cooler you've purchased explicitly for barbecue. Warning: This cooler will smell like barbecue forever, so you don't want to have brisket in it one week and beers the next. I have a cheap $20 cooler, and I put a disposable foil pan in the bottom of it to rest big cuts.

Central Texas–Style Smoked Brisket

———✳———

This is not a good place to start. A good place to start would be something that is harder to mess up, something like turkey breast (page 31) or sausage (page 27). **But brisket is king in Texas,** and so it comes first.

That said, mastering brisket is worth the time you put into it. Just ask Daniel Vaughn, who told me, "You should be able to do better than your local barbecue joint once you've gotten the principles down. You have just one brisket to focus on."

Traditionally, Central Texas barbecue is seasoned with just salt and pepper. You can go that route if you want, or add a tablespoon each of any/all of the following: paprika, chile powder, cumin, or granulated garlic powder. Your call. Do note that if you don't live in a barbecue region, you might have to call ahead and order a whole brisket from your butcher.

Smoking the brisket will take at least twelve hours plus time to rest, so please prepare accordingly. If I plan to serve a brisket at 7 p.m. for dinner, I take it out of the refrigerator at 5 a.m. that day. At the latest.

Serves 10 to 12.

2 tablespoons salt

2 tablespoons coarse-ground black pepper

1 packer-cut brisket (about 12 pounds/5.4 kg)

The night before you smoke the brisket, combine the salt, pepper, and optional seasonings together to prepare the rub. Trim the fat to between ¼ and ½ inch (6 and 12 mm) all over the brisket. Pat the meat dry and rub it generously with the seasoning, then set it on a sheet pan and cover it with plastic or foil. Refrigerate until morning.

On the day of the smoke, take the brisket out of the refrigerator and let it come to room temperature while you get the fire going.

Prepare a smoker to around 225°F (107°C). Once you've held it at that temperature for about 30 minutes, place the brisket directly on the grates of the smoker, fat side up, with the thicker end closer to the fire.

Leave it alone for a while, while keeping the smoker's temperature at 225°F (107°C). After a few hours, you can check it periodically to take the internal temperature of the brisket, but otherwise don't mess with it too much.

At first, the meat's temperature will rise pretty steadily. But at a certain point, you'll notice that the internal temperature of the brisket stops going up, somewhere around 160°F (71°C). This is called the stall. If you wrap the brisket at this point, it will help you get through the stall. (Some people consider this cheating. You can skip this step if you like, but it will take longer.) You can wrap the brisket in butcher paper, which is what the pros do, or you can wrap it in parchment paper (not waxed paper) or foil. Make sure it's fully wrapped, and put it back in the smoker.

Cook the brisket for several more hours, until the internal temperature of the meat reaches 200°F (93°C). Some pitmasters recommend going even higher, to 205°F (96°C), if you can wait that long.

Take the brisket off the smoker and let it rest for at least 1 hour at room temperature, or longer in a cooler or Cambro.

Slice and serve. With sauce (page 37) or not.

ZOMG BBQ
✳
WHILE THE BRISKET'S COOKING

"When you start, the brisket is limp. It would just fall over your hand as you pick it up. As it cooks, it starts to shrink and tighten up. It's pulling in that heat, that smoke, and it's getting real tight. It's kind of like if you were to step into a hot bath. You tense up at first, until you get used to the temperature, then you kind of loosen up.

You don't want any bounce back when you go to tap it. If you touch it and it's like a watermelon, you have a long time to go. If you can start to get a little press in, but it wants to give you a bounce back, you need to cook it a little longer. It's done when you're almost able to put your thumb through it."

—Lance Kirkpatrick, Stiles Switch

Smoked Sausage

You can smoke whatever kind of sausage you like, but the Texas hot guts sausage is traditional. This spicy, coarse-ground beef (and sometimes pork) sausage is the pride of Elgin, Texas, a small town just east of Austin. You can buy hot guts sausage from Elgin's Southside Market at many Texas grocery stores, or online directly from Southside. (If you're feeling feisty, make your own kielbasa, page 29.)

A properly smoked Texas **hot guts sausage snaps when you bite into it**—and drips grease down your forearms. Sausages are a great addition to the smoker when you're cooking a bigger piece of meat, like a brisket. They cook quickly, don't take up much room, and you can serve them to your hungry friends when they get antsy that the brisket's not done yet.

1 to 2 sausage links per person, either store-bought Texas hot guts sausage or From-Scratch Kielbasa (page 29)

Prepare a smoker to 250°F (120°C).

Smoke the sausages until their internal temperature reaches 160°F (71°C), about 1 hour. No need to flip. Rest them in a cooler if you're waiting on other meat to finish; otherwise they only need to rest for 10 minutes or so at room temperature before you can eat them.

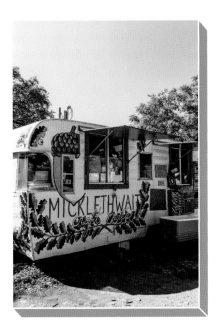

From-Scratch Kielbasa

Micklethwait Craft Meats

Tom Micklethwait and his crew smoke all kinds of meat, but this tiny, acorn-adorned trailer is known for its house-made sausages. These can range from pork belly andouille to jalapeño cheddar to good old-fashioned Texas hot links.

I'm partial to the kielbasa, a spicy sausage that mixes pork and beef. If you don't like it spicy you can skip the chile flakes, but make sure you include the curing salt, a necessary sausage ingredient you can buy online. Make sure your equipment and ingredients are super clean and chilled when making sausage.

Makes around 20 (6-inch/15-cm) sausage links.

4 pounds (1.8 kg) pork shoulder, cut into 1-inch (2.5-cm) chunks

1 pound (455 g) beef brisket, cut into 1-inch (2.5-cm) chunks

1½ tablespoons salt

½ teaspoon pink curing salt, such as Prague Powder No. 1

3 tablespoons coarse-ground black pepper

2 tablespoons minced garlic

1 tablespoon yellow mustard powder

½ teaspoon grated nutmeg

¼ teaspoon ginger powder

¼ cup finely chopped fresh sage

1 tablespoon red chile flakes

⅓ cup (75 ml) pineapple nectar (or substitute pineapple juice)

4 ounces (115 g) natural (hog) sausage casings

RECIPE CONTINUES ⟶

Place the meat in the freezer until thoroughly chilled but not frozen, about 30 minutes.

Combine the salt, curing salt, black pepper, garlic, mustard powder, nutmeg, ginger, sage, chile flakes, and pineapple nectar in a large bowl and add the meat, making sure the meat is thoroughly covered in the seasonings. Run the meat mixture through a meat grinder with a ¼-inch (6-mm) grinding disc, according to the manufacturer's instructions.

Prepare the casings: Run cold water through them to open them up and check for holes. Place them in a bowl of cold water.

Add about ½ cup (120 ml) cold water to a sheet pan and place it in front of a sausage stuffer. Fit one of the casings over the nozzle of the stuffer and put the meat mixture in the canister. Begin gently pushing the meat mixture through the stuffer, letting the stuffed sausage coil onto the sheet pan. When the casing is full, twist it off into 6-inch (15-cm) links. Repeat until you've used up the meat mixture.

Smoke according to the instructions on page 20. These sausages can also be boiled or roasted or grilled, as you wish.

ZOMG BBQ
✳

A BARBECUE LIBRARY

Texas-style pit smoking is a craft that takes time and practice to master. It is not learned in a day (or in a brief chapter in a cookbook). These are the very basics, and they'll get you started, but if you get serious about things you might consider taking a deeper dive into the genre. May I recommend the following books:

Franklin Barbecue:
A Meat-Smoking Manifesto,
by Aaron Franklin and
Jordan Mackay

Legends of Texas Barbecue
Cookbook, by Robb Walsh

Meathead: The Science of
Great Barbecue and Grilling,
by Meathead Goldwyn and
Greg Blonder

texasmonthly.com/bbq-home,
for Daniel Vaughn's insights into
the preparation of barbecue
as well as its history, and for
restaurant recommendations

Smoked Turkey

La Barbecue

The sleeper hit of barbecue, smoked turkey is more delicious than it has any right to be. You will be nervous about putting this bare turkey breast on your smoker, seemingly naked and destined to dry out, but don't be. Your turkey will end up juicy and delicious—Ali Clem, of La Barbecue, even says it's her favorite thing they serve.

Serves 6.

1 whole boneless turkey breast (3 to 4 pounds/.3 to 1.8 kg)

1 tablespoon salt

1 teaspoon black pepper

Prepare a smoker to 250°F (120°C).

Tuck the outside edges of each turkey lobe under to make a nice, round, uniform ball. Tie the ball with twine so it will smoke evenly.

Combine the salt and pepper in a small bowl and sprinkle the seasoning evenly over the turkey ball.

Once you've held the smoker at 250°F (120°C) for about 30 minutes, place the turkey in the smoker and cook until it reaches an internal temperature of 165°F (74°C), about 2 hours, or 30 minutes per pound (455 g). Let the smoked turkey rest for 30 minutes, then slice thinly and serve.

Ribs

Stiles Switch BBQ & Brew

Lance Kirkpatrick, pitmaster at Stiles Switch, acknowledges that "there are dozens if not hundreds of 'recipes' for pork ribs that mostly differ in the ingredients used for the rub, and whether the ribs are dry or wet." At Stiles Switch, he keeps it simple, and says this "ensures your best effort each time."

So go crazy with the rubs—or don't. Either way, this method will get you where you're going.

Makes as many ribs as you have hungry friends (or room on your smoker).

Salt

Black pepper

Pork ribs, your choice of cut (Stiles Switch uses spareribs)

Liberally salt and pepper both sides of the ribs and refrigerate overnight.

Prepare a smoker to 250°F (120°C).

Place the ribs bone side down, with the thicker end of the rack pointed toward the firebox. Cook for 1 hour, then turn the ribs so the thinner end of the ribs points toward the firebox. Cook for another 40 minutes, then turn again.

At this point, start checking the ribs every 20 minutes. You'll know they're done when they have some give— they'll flop over the side of a pair of tongs when you lift them off the pit.

Wrap the ribs and let them rest for at least 30 minutes before serving.

Note: Kirkpatrick recommends starting with a simple salt-and-pepper rub and then playing with chili powder, garlic, paprika, and flavored salts. If you like a wet rib, he recommends spritzing the ribs with apple cider vinegar or apple juice during cooking. If you like sweet ribs, try sprinkling with brown sugar toward the end of the cook—if you do it at the beginning, the sugar will burn.

Smoked Pork Shoulder

Kerlin BBQ

Pork shoulder is not traditionally associated with Texas barbecue. But Bill Kerlin, of Kerlin BBQ, makes his as Texan as he can: "No crazy rubs, no injections, no marinating, just salt and pepper. ***Just keep it simple.***"

Kerlin mixes the pulled pork with simple pan drippings instead of barbecue sauce, so you can revel in the pure joy of meat seasoned with only salt, pepper, and smoke.

Serves 10 to 12.

¼ cup (75 g) salt

½ cup (55 g) black pepper

1 bone-in pork butt (8 to 10 pounds/ 3.6 to 4.5 kg)

¼ cup (60 ml) vegetable oil

Mix the salt and pepper together. Lightly coat the pork with oil and then rub the salt-and-pepper mixture all over it. Refrigerate the meat for at least 3 hours, but ideally overnight.

Prepare a smoker to 275°F (135°C).

Place the pork in the smoker with the fat cap up. Smoke for 4 to 5 hours, or until a bark forms over the surface of the meat and the fat cap splits. You should be able to see some of the lighter-colored fat peeking through the crack.

At this point, place the pork in an aluminum pan, cover it with foil, and seal. (The pan allows you to catch the drippings.) Return it to the pit and cook until the meat is soft and the bone pulls away easily; the internal temperature of the meat will be about 205°F (96°C).

Let the pork rest, covered, for 30 to 45 minutes, or until cool enough to handle.

Pull or chop the pork, discarding any large pieces of fat that haven't rendered, and mix the meat with the drippings from the pan.

On the Side

Smoked meat is definitely the star of the barbecue show, but it always helps to have a few killer sides in your pocket, too. You'll want sliced pickles, sliced white onion, and white bread available for your guests, as well as barbecue sauce for those who like it. You may also want slices of cheddar cheese, pickled jalapeños, and hot sauce, especially if people are making sandwiches.

Potato salad and coleslaw are probably the most common prepared sides. You might also see beans, macaroni and cheese (page 111), corn dishes, greens, and other salads made with cucumbers or green beans. Here are some of the best sides the Austin barbecue world has to offer—bring any of these to a pal's cookout and you'll be sure to get invited back.

Barbecue Sauce

This is how I make barbecue sauce when I'm not thinking about it too hard. It's just the right combination of spicy, sweet, and tangy without going over the top—perfect for showcasing that meat you worked so hard on. (For an even simpler version, check out the sauce that goes with Jacoby's Meatloaf, on page 118.)

Makes about 2 quarts (2 L). You can freeze the leftovers for your next barbecue.

4 tablespoons (115 g) unsalted butter

1 cup (125 g) finely chopped onion

4 garlic cloves, finely chopped

1 large can (7 ounces/199 g) whole chipotle peppers in adobo sauce, chopped, sauce reserved

1 can (28 ounces/794 g) crushed tomatoes

1 beer (12 ounces/360 ml) of your choice

½ cup (120 ml) ketchup

¼ cup (60 ml) apple cider vinegar

¼ cup (55 g) brown sugar

Salt and black pepper

In a medium saucepan over medium heat, melt the butter. Add the onion and garlic and sauté until the onion is translucent, about 5 minutes. Add the chipotles, reserved chipotle sauce, tomatoes, beer, ketchup, vinegar, and brown sugar. Bring to a boil, then lower the heat to a simmer. Simmer the sauce to let the flavors combine (and cook the alcohol off) until slightly thickened, about 20 minutes. Season with salt and black pepper to taste.

Note: If you like, you can mix the meat drippings from your barbecue into the sauce as well.

Brisket Frito Pie

Stiles Switch BBQ & Brew

The Frito pie is a thing of great and humble beauty: basic corn chips topped with (in this case) brisket, beans, and cheese. Feel free to go nuts with the toppings—avocado is good, as is chopped cilantro, hot sauce, or anything else you'd put on nachos. ***The Frito pie may be humble, but restrained it is not.***

Serves 2 to 4 as an appetizer, or 1 really hungry person as a main.

1 cup (150–200 g) chopped smoked brisket (page 24) or other leftover barbecue

¼ cup (60 ml) barbecue sauce (page 37)

2 cups (60 g) Fritos corn chips

½ cup (85 g) cooked pinto beans (page 42)

¼ cup (30 g) shredded cheddar cheese

¼ cup (35 g) finely chopped onion

¼ cup (35 g) sliced pickled jalapeños (page 226 or store-bought)

Mix the brisket and sauce together.

<u>**Note**</u>: Sometimes you'll see this mixture on Texas barbecue menus as "chopped beef."

Place the Fritos in the bottom of a shallow bowl. Top the chips with beans first, then the chopped beef, then the cheese. Add a sprinkle of onion and pickled jalapeños and serve.

Chipotle Slaw

La Barbecue

Spicy, smoky, and orange, this chipotle slaw is as iconic as La Barbecue's meats. Well, almost. You'll want to make this ahead of time so it can chill for a bit, but make it the same day you plan to serve it or it will get soggy.

Makes 1 large, party-size bowl, about 10 cups (2.4 L).

1 cup (240 ml) mayonnaise

1 small can (3½ ounces/100 g, or about ⅓ cup/75 ml) whole or diced chipotle peppers in adobo sauce

1 teaspoon paprika

1 teaspoon salt

1 teaspoon granulated garlic powder

2 teaspoons black pepper

1 head green cabbage, quartered, cored, and thinly sliced (about 6 cups/565 g)

½ head purple cabbage, quartered, cored, and thinly sliced (about 3 cups/280 g)

2 carrots, peeled and grated (about 1 cup/110 g)

In a food processor or blender, blend the mayonnaise, chipotles and their sauce, paprika, salt, granulated garlic, and black pepper until smooth.

Combine the cabbages and carrots in a large bowl. Add the dressing and toss until the vegetables are coated. Refrigerate until thoroughly chilled, at least 1 hour. Serve cold.

Jalapeño Cheese Grits

Micklethwait Craft Meats

Grits aren't necessarily a traditional side for Texas barbecue, but who cares when they're this good? These grits get their flavor from mellowing chopped jalapeños in a combination of butter, cream cheese, and gorgonzola. Super decadent, they're easily one of the most beloved barbecue sides in town.

Serves 6 to 8 as a side.

6 tablespoons (85 g) unsalted butter

4 ounces (115 g) cream cheese

2 ounces (55 g) gorgonzola cheese

10 jalapeños, stemmed, seeded, and chopped

5 cups (1.2 L) vegetable or chicken stock

3 cups (720 ml) half-and-half

Salt

2 cups (275 g) coarse-ground yellow grits

1 cup (115 g) shredded sharp cheddar cheese

In a large pot over low heat, melt the butter, cream cheese, and gorgonzola together, stirring constantly. Add the jalapeños and cook until softened, about 5 minutes.

Add the stock and half-and-half and bring to a simmer. Add a good-size pinch of salt.

Add the grits gradually, stirring constantly to prevent lumps. Return to a simmer, stir in the cheddar, and cover. Remove from the heat. Let rest, with the lid on, for 20 minutes. Season to taste and serve.

Traditional Pinto Beans

Stiles Switch BBQ & Brew

This is a basic recipe for pinto beans from Stiles Switch. You can swap out the pintos for another variety of beans—black beans are nice—and replace the chile powder with whatever seasonings or spice blends you like. Cooked, crumbled bacon or, as noted below, leftover barbecue makes a fine addition too. These beans are the base for the refried beans (page 76) in the Tex-Mex chapter, and a necessary ingredient in Frito pie (page 38).

Serves 6 to 8 as a side.

1 pound (455 g) dried pinto beans

2 tablespoons vegetable oil

1 cup (110 g) chopped onion

2 tablespoons granulated garlic powder

2 tablespoons New Mexico (Anaheim) chile powder

1 teaspoon ground cayenne

1 cup (125 g) chopped smoked brisket (page 24; optional)

Salt

Sort through the beans and rinse them well.

Heat a Dutch oven or heavy pot over medium heat and add the oil. Add the onion and cook until translucent, 3 to 5 minutes. Add the granulated garlic, chile powder, and cayenne, and sauté until fragrant, about 1 minute more.

Add the rinsed and drained beans to the pot and cover them with water by a couple of inches. Bring to a boil, then lower the heat to a simmer. Cook, partially covered, until the beans are tender and the liquid is slightly thickened, about 2 hours. If using the brisket, add it to the pot about 30 minutes before the beans are done. Season with salt to taste and serve.

Jalapeño Dill Potato Salad

Kerlin BBQ

It's pretty common to serve potato salad with Texas barbecue, but this isn't really a typical potato salad. While it keeps the traditional mayonnaise base, the addition of pickled jalapeños, dill, and scallions does a lot to perk up this salad, making it a hit at parties.

Bill Kerlin explains, "Originally we had started with a mustard potato salad, which was good. But it was just too common. The idea for the jalapeño and dill was because that's what we were growing in our garden." While it's plenty tempting to eat this right when it's done, don't skip the chilling step—it makes the dish.

Makes 1 large party-size bowl, about 10 cups (2.4 L).

5 pounds (2.3 kg) red potatoes, skin on

Salt

1 cup (240 ml) sour cream

1 cup (240 ml) mayonnaise

Black pepper

2 bunches scallions, thinly sliced

1 cup (50 g) chopped fresh dill

1 cup (140 g) chopped pickled jalapeños (page 226 or store-bought)

Put the potatoes in a pot full of cold, salted water. Bring the water to a boil and cook the potatoes until they are soft, about 20 minutes. Drain, then let cool to room temperature. Cut the potatoes into ½-inch (12-mm) cubes.

In a small bowl, whisk the sour cream and mayonnaise together. Season this dressing to taste with salt and pepper.

Combine the potatoes, scallions, dill, and jalapeños in a large bowl and mix well, then pour the dressing over the vegetables. Toss just until the dressing is evenly distributed.

Chill in the refrigerator overnight, ideally, or until thoroughly chilled, at least 1 hour. Serve cold.

CHAPTER

TACOS

Taco Town

Everyone—everyone—in Austin is fueled by tacos.

Pretty much anything tastes good wrapped in a tortilla, and people here take advantage of that. Tacos can be vegetarian, gluten-free, vegan, or loaded with chicken-fried you-name-it and topped with queso. They can be super-traditional Mexican tacos, crispy old-school Tex-Mex tacos, tricked-out amped-up tacos, or something else altogether. They can be the eggy glory that is the breakfast taco (see the breakfast chapter, page 155).

Austin didn't invent tacos, of course, and there are certainly other cities in Texas that boast incredible taquerias. But tacos are nevertheless part of the fabric of this city, to the point where it's almost possible to take them for granted. You don't go out for tacos, you "grab" them, like they're just hanging from a tree in your front yard. Like you can stick your hand out of a moving vehicle and pluck foil-wrapped, tortilla-bound GOODNESS from thin air as you drive down the street. (Heck, if the place has a drive-thru, you sort of can.)

They are omnipresent, popping up where you least expect them. I have eaten fantastic tacos at gas stations and Laundromats, and, once, outside my polling place in the hallway of a local elementary school.

The tacos in this chapter represent a spectrum of Austin's taco offerings, from the traditional (Tamale House East's Traditional Carne Molida Tacos, page 55) to the new school (the Peached Tortilla's Banh Mi Tacos, page 61). There are also tacos in the breakfast chapter (page 155). And whatever taco you decide to make, remember: If it fits in a tortilla, it'll probably TASTE GOOD in one. Don't take that for granted.

Corn or Flour?

Which tortilla goes best with which taco? The short, simple answer is whichever you prefer. If you love flour tortillas, go with your heart. If you're into corn, follow your bliss. Alternately, go with whichever is higher quality: If there's a store around the corner from your house that makes fresh corn tortillas, go with those over those odd, shiny flour tortillas you get in the bread aisle at the supermarket.

    A slightly more philosophical answer is that corn tortillas are best when you want the tortilla to soak up some juice. That's why they're really the only tortilla you should use for enchiladas. (Ever had flour tortilla enchiladas? Slimy is putting it kindly.) Thus, corn tortillas work well with carnitas and barbacoa, whereas flour tortillas are great with breakfast tacos.

To Heat Tortillas

Unless you just made your tortillas fresh, they're going to need to be heated before you can use them for tacos. There are a few ways to do this, and none of them involve the microwave, which will turn your tortillas to mush.

Both corn and flour tortillas do well in a dry skillet or cast-iron pan over medium heat for about 30 seconds on each side. Corn tortillas will get crispy if you heat them in a little oil—a few seconds per side in hot oil will result in crispy-yet-pliable tortillas, while a bath in a couple inches of hot oil for about 1 minute will get you the school lunch–style crispy taco shells of your dreams. (Bend the tortillas into that classic U-shape using tongs while they fry.)

If you're making tacos for a big group or party, wrap stacks of eight tortillas in foil and put the stacks in a 300°F (150°C) oven for 10 minutes. You can then hold them (but not for long) in plastic or fabric tortilla warmers, available at restaurant supply stores, Mexican grocery stores, and online.

Braised Pig Tail Puffy Tacos

Swift's Attic

Puffy tacos are pretty much what they sound like: fresh masa rolled thin and fried until, well, puffy. The degree of puffiness can vary anywhere from slightly thicker than a traditional crunchy taco shell to all-the-way puffed up, like a ball. A phenomenon more commonly associated with regions south of Austin—specifically San Antonio—puffy tacos do make their way into the capital city here and there.

These are not traditional puffy tacos, fitting the playful food at Swift's Attic. The masa shells are smaller than usual, about three inches (7.5 cm) across, making these more happy-hour bites than a full meal. They're great for parties, since everything can be prepped in advance—heat the shells on a baking sheet in a 300°F oven just before guests arrive.

Makes about 24 mini-tacos. Serves 6.

1 recipe crispy masa shells (recipe follows)

1 recipe braised pork tails (see Note)

Grapefruit Salsa (page 225)

Top each masa shell with about 2 tablespoons meat; dress with salsa to taste.

<u>**Note**</u>: Prepare the Basic Braised Pork (page 51) for tacos, substituting 5 pounds (2.3 kg) pig tails for pork shoulder. You may also add ¼ cup (55 g) light brown sugar, 1 tablespoon hot paprika, 2 teaspoons ground cumin, and 1 teaspoon ground coriander to the seasoning.

Crispy Masa Shells

3 cups (340 g) masa flour
½ tablespoon salt
2 teaspoons baking powder
2¼ cups (540 ml) warm water
Vegetable oil for deep-frying

Mix the masa flour, salt, baking powder, and water together until a dough forms; scoop the dough into 2-tablespoon balls. Flatten the balls into round discs about 3 inches (7.5 cm) across, and chill for at least 1 hour.

Heat a couple inches of oil in a deep pot to 350°F (175°C), or until a small piece of dough dropped in the oil sizzles immediately. Fry the discs until golden brown, 1 to 2 minutes per side. Remove to a paper towel to drain.

Basic Braised Pork for Tacos

This is a very basic pork braise that will result in pulled pork for tacos. You can use this method in several recipes in this book, including the Braised Pig Tail Puffy Tacos (page 49) and the Texas Benedict (page 169). It's also good as enchilada filling.

In the same way that you can play around with rubs in barbecue, feel free to add small amounts of chile powder, paprika, onion powder, granulated garlic powder, or whatever seasonings you like to the spice rub. (Some people add brown sugar to rubs; if you do this, be very careful not to burn the pork when browning.)

Makes 4 quarts (3.8 L) of taco filling (which is a lot, but it freezes well).

1 pork shoulder (about 8 pounds/ 3.6 kg), cut into 3-inch (7.5-cm) cubes

¼ cup (60 g) salt

¼ cup (28 g) black pepper

3 tablespoons vegetable oil

Rub the pork with the salt and pepper and refrigerate it overnight, or for at least 1 hour.

Heat the oven to 300°F (150°C).

Heat the oil in a large Dutch oven. Working in batches, brown the pork. When all of the meat is browned, put it back in the Dutch oven along with any drippings that may have collected, and add water to cover by an inch (2.5 cm) or so. Cover the pot, bring to a simmer, and transfer to the oven to braise until the pork is incredibly tender, 4 to 5 hours, checking periodically to make sure the meat is covered with liquid. (If it's not, add more water.) Let the meat cool in its braising liquid, then lightly pull the meat, discarding gristle-y bits and unrendered fat.

When you're ready to make tacos, you can reheat small amounts of the braised meat in its liquid in a saucepan until warmed through; remove the meat with a slotted spoon and serve. For a crispier taco filling, heat the drained meat in a sauté pan over medium heat with a small amount of oil until it just begins to brown and crisp up.

Carne Asada Tacos

Tacodeli

Tacodeli is a growing taco shop with South Austin roots, and they are committed to serving local and organic foods wherever they can. They serve a wide variety of tacos, from traditional options like the carne asada tacos here to their own creations—mashed potato breakfast tacos, anyone? And if the line out the door at lunchtime tells you anything, the tacos are pretty tasty.

These carne asada tacos represent what Tacodeli does best: high-quality ingredients, prepared simply. You can make these outside on the grill or inside on the stove, whichever you prefer.

Serves 4.

¼ cup (35 g) finely diced onion

¼ cup (10 g) finely chopped fresh cilantro

2 teaspoons paprika

2 teaspoons salt

2 teaspoons black pepper

2 ribeye steaks (½ inch/12 mm thick)

1 tablespoon vegetable oil

Corn or flour tortillas

2 limes, cut into wedges

2 avocados, sliced

Salsa (see chapter 9)

Combine the onion and cilantro and set aside. (Tacodeli calls this ubiquitous taco garnish "mex-mix.")

Mix the paprika, salt, and pepper together and rub the mixture all over the steaks. Heat a skillet over high heat, add the oil, and sear the steaks on both sides. You don't need to cook it all the way to your preferred doneness—you'll cook it more right before you serve it. Just cook it long enough to get a good sear on the meat, 1 to 2 minutes per side. Remove the steak to a cutting board and let it rest for 15 minutes.

Cut the steak into ½-inch (12-mm) dice, discarding any unrendered fat, and return it to the skillet over medium heat. Sauté until cooked to your preferred doneness, about 2 minutes for medium-rare. Heat the tortillas (see page 49) and serve the tacos with a lime wedge, sliced avocado, the cilantro-onion mix, and your choice of salsa.

Old-School Carne Molida Tacos

Tamale House East

Several locations of Tamale House have come and gone since the original restaurant closed in 1984, but each one has been run by the descendants of Moses "Baby Moe" Vasquez. The family's dishes have been passed down thanks to Vasquez's daughter Diane, who started working in the family business at age thirteen; her daughter Carmen Valera calls her "the guardian of the recipes." Today, several of Vasquez's grandchildren, including Valera, run Tamale House East on East Sixth Street, where they serve these old-school crispy beef tacos that were on the menu at the original location.

Valera says the key to making these tacos like her grandfather did is to use yellow corn tortillas (the white ones will fall apart) and fry them lightly in oil: "Not until hard, and not soft, either. They are kind of medium; you want them to have enough bend that you can fold them without cracking them in half." For the true Baby Moe experience, dress them with Louisiana Hot Sauce: Valera says he carried a small bottle of it in his shirt pocket wherever he went. (She herself prefers Crystal.)

Makes 10 to 12 tacos.

RECIPE CONTINUES ⟶

For the carne molida

- 2 pounds (910 g) ground beef (a fatty blend, like 80/20)
- 1 medium onion, diced (about 1 cup / 110 g)
- 4 tablespoons (37 g) granulated garlic powder
- 2 tablespoons ground cumin
- 1 teaspoon black pepper
- 1 cup (240 g) whole, peeled tomatoes and their juices (canned)
- 1 tablespoon salt

Put the ground beef and diced onions in a pot with ½ cup (120 ml) water; stir to combine. Cover, bring to a boil, and then reduce to barely a simmer. Add the garlic powder, cumin, black pepper, tomatoes, and salt to the meat. Stir to combine, then simmer for an hour and a half, stirring occasionally while breaking up the tomatoes with a spoon. If the mixture dries out, add a little more water as it cooks. You're not searing anything; the idea is to have super-soft meat.

For the crispy tacos

- Vegetable oil for frying
- 10 to 12 yellow corn tortillas (or store-bought crispy taco shells)
- 1 tomato, chopped
- 1 cup (55 g) shredded lettuce or spinach
- Shredded cheddar cheese
- Guacamole (page 75)
- Hot sauce

If using fresh tortillas, add a few tablespoons of oil to a skillet, enough to cover the bottom of the pan. Fry the tortillas over medium heat one at a time until they are slightly crispy but still pliable, 1 minute or so on each side. Serve the meat in the tortillas immediately, with tomato, lettuce, cheese, guacamole, and your choice of hot sauce.

Chicken Tinga

Jack Allen's Kitchen

This is the filling for the Enchiladas Tejanas (page 88), but it also makes for a great taco.

Serves 6.

1 whole chicken (3 to 4 pounds/1.4 to 1.8 kg), or 1 cooked rotisserie chicken

Salt

2 tablespoons adobo sauce from a can of chipotle peppers

2 cups (360 g) diced tomatoes

1 cup (110 g) diced red onion

3 medium jalapeños, seeded and diced

2 tablespoons chopped fresh cilantro

Juice of 1 lime

If using a raw chicken: Heat the oven to 400°F (205°C). Salt the chicken liberally, and roast in a pan or cast-iron skillet until the juices run clear or the internal temperature hits 165°F (74°C), about 1 hour 15 minutes. Let the chicken cool completely.

Shred the cooked or rotisserie chicken meat into a pot, removing skin and bones and chewy bits. (You can save the bones for making stock, if you like.) Add the adobo sauce, tomatoes, onion, jalapeño, cilantro, and lime. Bring to a boil, reduce the heat to a simmer, and simmer for about 5 minutes, or until the vegetables have released their liquid. Remove from the heat and season to taste.

Tacos de Hongos

You can use whatever mushrooms are available, although I like to use a mixture of a few different kinds when possible. The key to these is getting the pan blazing hot, so a cast-iron skillet works best if you have one.

Serves 6.

For the hongos

1 tablespoon vegetable oil

1 poblano pepper, stem and seeds removed, cut into thin strips

½ small onion, thinly sliced

Salt and black pepper

8 ounces (225 g) mushrooms, cut into ¼-inch (6-mm) slices

Heat a skillet until very hot, nearly smoking. Add the oil and immediately add the poblano and onion and season with salt and black pepper. Cook, stirring constantly, until the vegetables begin to soften and brown on the edges, 3 to 5 minutes. Remove the pepper and onion to a plate, and repeat the process with the mushrooms, cooking until the edges just start to brown. Combine the cooked mushrooms with the pepper and onion.

For the tacos

Corn or flour tortillas

¼ cup (30 g) crumbled Cotija cheese

Lime wedges

Hot sauce or salsa (see chapter 9)

Heat the tortillas (see page 48) and serve with the hot filling, a sprinkling of cheese, a squirt of lime, and hot sauce or salsa.

Banh Mi Tacos

The Peached Tortilla

The Peached Tortilla was founded by Eric Silverstein in 2010—an early entrant in Austin's food truck boom—serving Asian-inspired mash-ups like these banh mi tacos. What began as a single roaming food truck now also encompasses a brick-and-mortar restaurant and an event space. These tacos combine a five-spice braised pork belly with banh mi toppings, all wrapped up in a tortilla.

Makes 8 to 10 tacos.

Braised pork belly (recipe follows)
Corn or flour tortillas
Pickled daikon and carrots (recipe follows)
Sriracha mayonnaise (recipe follows)
Fresh cilantro

Heat a pan over high heat and add the chopped pork belly; sauté until the meat is slightly crisped and heated through. Heat the tortillas (see page 48). Put the pork in the tortillas and top with pickled daikon and carrots, sriracha mayonnaise, and cilantro.

Pickled Daikon and Carrots

1 small daikon (about 8 ounces/225 g), peeled and cut into thin strips

3 carrots (about 8 ounces/225 g total), peeled and grated

2 tablespoons rice vinegar

2 tablespoons chili garlic sauce

1 tablespoon fish sauce

3 tablespoons sugar

Mix all the ingredients together and chill thoroughly, about 1 hour and up to 2 days.

Sriracha Mayo

½ cup (120 ml) mayonnaise

3 tablespoons sriracha

1 tablespoon fresh lemon juice

1 tablespoon rice vinegar

Whisk all the ingredients together until smooth. Store in the refrigerator.

Wild Boar: The Delicious Menace

Chef Jesse Griffiths of Dai Due doesn't just run a butcher shop and restaurant, he also teaches classes on the responsible use of wild Texas resources. These days, that often means focusing on how to deal with the state's infestation of wild boar. He explains:

Half the population of feral hogs in the United States resides in Texas, every county in Texas—that's 254 counties. From the Sabine to El Paso, Amarillo to Brownsville: they're everywhere.

But luckily, you can eat them.

If the hog's got a fair amount of fat on it, you can use it pretty much anywhere you'd use farmed pork. In fact, some of the most beautiful pork I've ever seen is from feral hogs. Hogs from San Saba especially look like domesticated pork, because they're eating pecans and acorns and probably a little corn, too. They have a fat cap on them, they're a little marbled, they're fantastic.

I could have a very compelling conversation with a vegan as to why you should eat feral hogs. They're killing your vegetables, they're polluting the rivers, they're destroying farmland, outcompeting native species, killing ground-nesting birds. People think the quail decline of recent years might be related to feral hogs. If we don't do anything about them at all, then we're going to have an ecological disaster.

So we hunt them, we trap them a little bit. It's mostly standard rifle hunting. I enjoy it. We kill every hog that we see, and use all their meat. That's why we focus on them so heavily, trying to educate people about what can be done with them.

Think about it this way: if a farmer kills two boars that are destroying his crops, and instead of leaving them in a field, he takes them and butchers them, he has a hundred pounds of meat in his freezer. That's a hundred fewer pounds of intensively farmed meat that has to be produced.

When the Spaniards landed in Texas in the sixteenth century, they brought their hogs. When they were exploring, they'd drop a pair of pigs off, knowing that at some point they're going to come back. A pair of hogs is going to reproduce, and when they come back, there'd be pigs. They were planted like little seeds here in Texas.

Fast-forward to the twentieth century. There's been a real explosion. Exponential population booms twenty years ago, five years ago, two years ago. They breed at an incredible rate. The whole cycle is catastrophic. If you've ever seen the damage they do—they can devastate a field of crops. It looks like bombs went off: they dig huge pits. You'll sprain your ankle!

And they'll eat anything. They'll eat baby deer, quail, turkeys, crops, grubs, roots, anything. They're very adaptive, intelligent, and have a really good sense of smell. They're survivors. That's what makes them so hard to control. They will come at you if they're cornered. I respect the hell out of them. But I've seen what they can do to two acres of crops overnight. It's devastating.

CHAPTER

TEX-MEX

AND

INTERIOR

MEXICAN

From Tex to Mex
(and Everything in Between)

From cheese enchiladas to intricate Oaxacan-style moles, Austinites of Mexican heritage have had a tremendous impact on the way this city eats. Generation after generation has influenced and changed not just the Mexican food served here, but Austin dining as a whole. Today the city boasts a wide range of Tex-Mex, Mexican, and Mexican-influenced restaurants.

On one end of the spectrum is poor, misunderstood Tex-Mex, the Texas-born regional cuisine that highlights the many delicious uses of melty yellow cheese, chile con carne, and flour tortillas. On the other end, the term *interior Mexican* refers to the many regional cuisines of Mexico and includes foods like tacos al pastor, cochinita pibil, and the aforementioned moles. Austin is lucky to be home to two giants of each cuisine: Matt's El Rancho, one of the great Tex-Mex institutions, and Fonda San Miguel, one of the premier interior Mexican restaurants in the country.

Matt and Janie Martinez opened Matt's El Rancho in 1952. Now run by their children, Matt's El Rancho still makes tortillas in house. The most famous dish at Matt's El Rancho is, undoubtedly, the Bob Armstrong Dip (page 70), a tricked-out queso topped with guacamole and spiced ground beef. But the restaurant is famous for more than just Bob dip: Their chile relleno is renowned (and was reportedly President Johnson's favorite food), as are their fajitas and old-fashioned tacos. Not to mention the margaritas.

In part a response to the Tex-Mex dishes served across Austin and the rest of Texas, Tom Gilliland and the late Miguel Ravago opened Fonda San Miguel in 1975 to focus on interior Mexican dishes. Championed by none other than legendary cookbook author Diana Kennedy, Fonda San Miguel has become famous for its epic Sunday brunch buffet, its tequila and mezcal lists, and signature entrées like chiles en nogada and the chipotle-rubbed grilled lamb chops shared later in this chapter (page 82). The restaurant is also known for its art collection, featuring artists like Juan Torres Calderón, Francisco Zúñiga, and Rufino Tamayo, as well as folk art from all over Mexico.

These restaurants may serve very different menus, but the Austin restaurant world of today couldn't exist without either of them. Restaurants here don't often fall neatly into the categories of either Tex-Mex or interior Mexican, instead happily drawing inspiration from both traditions.

It's not uncommon to order a bowl of chips and queso followed by an entrée of cochinita pibil, or to see frozen strawberry margaritas listed on a menu next to an extensive selection of mezcals. And to our great benefit, these cuisines continue to evolve and cross-pollinate.

Bob Armstrong Dip

Matt's El Rancho

Former Texas land commisioner Bob Armstrong was a Matt's El Rancho regular. Apparently bored of the typical menu offerings, legend has it Armstrong asked Matt Martinez Jr. to make something up just for him. Martinez added a scoop of beef taco meat and a scoop of guacamole to the restaurant's queso, and **Tex-Mex history was made**. Armstrong died in 2015, but he's still on a first-name basis with Matt's El Rancho diners, who order small Bobs and large Bobs every day.

You can make any of these three components separately, if you like, or make a vegetarian Bob by swapping the beef for some pinto beans (page 42). Serve this with tortilla chips.

Makes 1 large Bob, with a bit of leftover meat and guac. Serves 6.

For the meat

- 8 ounces (225 g) ground beef
- ¼ cup (35 g) finely diced red bell pepper
- ¼ cup (35 g) finely diced onion
- 1 stalk celery, finely diced
- ½ teaspoon granulated garlic powder
- ½ teaspoon ground cumin
- 1 teaspoon salt
- 1 teaspoon black pepper

Heat a pot over medium heat, then add all the ingredients. Cook, stirring, until the onion is translucent and the meat is cooked, about 5 minutes. Most of the liquid should evaporate, but the mixture shouldn't be dry. Keep warm while you prepare the other components.

For the guacamole

- 2 ripe avocados, peeled, pits removed
- Juice of ½ lemon
- ½ teaspoon granulated garlic powder
- 1 tablespoon vegetable oil
- 1 small Roma tomato, finely diced
- Salt

Combine the avocados, lemon juice, granulated garlic, and oil, mashing everything slightly. The mixture should be chunky, not smooth. Stir in the tomato and season with salt.

For the queso

- 1 stalk celery, finely diced
- ¼ cup (35 g) finely diced red bell pepper
- ¼ cup (35 g) finely diced white onion
- ½ cup (75 g) diced poblano pepper
- ½ cup (90 g) diced Roma tomato
- 2 cups (225 g) shredded or cubed American cheese (processed cheese will work in a pinch)

Bring 1 cup (240 ml) water to a boil in a small saucepan. Add the celery, bell pepper, onion, poblano, and tomato and boil briefly to cook everything, about 1 minute. Turn the heat down to low, and gradually whisk in the cheese. Heat for a few minutes, stirring constantly. The second all the cheese is melted and everything is heated through and smooth, remove from the heat so it doesn't overcook. Do this step right before serving: If you used American cheese the dip will separate as it cools; if you used processed cheese it will develop a skin on top as it sits.

Pour the hot queso into a wide, shallow serving bowl. Add a scoop of meat and a scoop of guacamole, about ½ cup (120 ml) of each. Do not mix. Guests should combine the queso, guacamole, and ground beef together with tortilla chips as they eat it.

TRIVIA
*
BOB ARMSTRONG'S OTHER NAMESAKE

Believe it or not, queso isn't the only thing named after beloved statesman Bob Armstrong. Thanks to his role in convincing the state to purchase a 300,000-acre ranch on the Texas-Mexico border—including its eight-mile-wide collapsed ancient volcano—the visitor center at Big Bend Ranch State Park has been named in his honor.

What Is Tex-Mex?

Tex-Mex gets a bad rap. Outside of Texas, it's almost a dirty word: It's used to mean fast food or substandard, Americanized "Mexican." But ask any former Austinite who has moved out of state what they miss most about living here, and the answer is not going to be the bluebonnets. Half of those Tex-pats will dreamily sigh about queso, while the rest will swoon over memories of migas tacos. Or, heck, just a decent tortilla.

Why? Since it's so hard to get good Tex-Mex outside of Texas, it's the definition of home for lots of Texans. Dishes like crispy tacos (pages 55–56), Chile con Carne Enchiladas (page 79), or queso made with processed cheese (page 72) are maddeningly underappreciated in the rest of the country.

The key to understanding Tex-Mex is to stop thinking about it as a variation on Mexican food. There are similarities, but Tex-Mex is an American regional cuisine that was born and raised in Texas. Cookbook author Robb Walsh argues in his *Tex-Mex Cookbook* that the roots of Tex-Mex can be traced to the nineteenth-century chili queens of San Antonio—and even further back, when eighteenth-century immigrants from the Canary Islands brought their love of cumin with them to Texas.

But Tex-Mex as we know it today, with its bowls of neon-orange queso and combo platters, evolved in the twentieth century. *Texas Monthly* food editor Pat Sharpe notes in a 2003 article, "Classic Tex-Mex was born in Texas in the Mexican restaurants run by first- and second-generation immigrants during the first third of the twentieth century. It peaked in a kind of golden age (the color of melted Velveeta, no doubt) that lasted roughly from World War II to the Vietnam War."

Indeed, many of Austin's Tex-Mex restaurants—including Matt's El Rancho, Maudie's, and Joe's Bakery—have been in business since the mid-twentieth century and remain open today. Tex-Mex continues to evolve, blending with interior Mexican as more recent Mexican transplants bring their traditions to Texas, and taking cues from modern restaurant trends.

But no matter what happens, we'll always have queso.

Guacamole

Second Bar + Kitchen

This ever-so-slightly dressed up guacamole comes via veteran Austin chef David Bull, whose Second Bar + Kitchen now has a few popular locations. The red onion and cilantro give this guacamole a little more jazz than the super-simple version used for the Bob Armstrong Dip (page 70), and it's spiked with a bit of red wine vinegar for added depth.

Makes 1 medium bowl of guacamole, about 2 cups (480 ml).

4 small ripe avocados

¼ cup (45 g) finely diced tomato

¼ cup (35 g) finely diced red onion

2 teaspoons minced fresh cilantro

½ jalapeño, minced

½ teaspoon red wine vinegar

Juice of ½ lime, or more to taste

2 teaspoons coarse salt, or more to taste

Mash the avocado in a bowl, leaving it a little bit chunky. Add the remaining ingredients, including additional lime juice or salt if you prefer, and stir to combine. Serve immediately.

Rice and Beans

You cannot have Tex-Mex without rice and beans. There are probably as many recipes for rice and beans as there are Tex-Mex restaurants in Austin, but this is how I make them.

Serves 6 as a side.

For the restaurant-style rice

1 tablespoon vegetable oil

3 garlic cloves, minced

½ cup (65 g) finely diced onion

1 tablespoon tomato paste

1 cup (185 g) long-grain white rice

2 cups (480 ml) chicken stock or water

½ teaspoon ground cumin

1 teaspoon salt

Heat the oil in a pot over medium heat. Add the garlic and onion and cook until the onion is translucent, 3 to 5 minutes. Add the tomato paste and rice and cook for another minute, stirring constantly so the tomato paste doesn't burn.

Add the stock and stir until the tomato paste dissolves. Add the cumin and salt and bring to a boil. Cover, reduce the heat to a simmer, and cook without removing the lid for 20 minutes. If there's still liquid in the pot after 20 minutes, remove from the heat and let the rice rest for 10 minutes with the lid on—it should soak up the rest of the liquid. Fluff the rice with a fork.

For the refried beans

2 tablespoons lard or bacon grease (or, if you must, vegetable oil)

3 garlic cloves, minced

3 cups (515 g) cooked pinto beans (page 42 or store-bought), drained, 1 cup (240 ml) cooking liquid reserved

Salt

Melt the lard in a large skillet over medium heat. Add the garlic and cook until you can smell it, about 1 minute, then add beans with about ½ cup (120 ml) of their liquid. Mash the beans with the back of a spoon or a potato masher until you've gotten all of them, more or less—it doesn't need to be perfectly smooth. Add some of the beans' cooking liquid until you reach your desired consistency, then season with salt. Serve with the rice.

Green Chile Queso

Queso is an infinitely customizable dish. I like my queso popping with roasted green chiles and with a teensy bit of "real" cheese (i.e., not processed cheese) to give it those camera-ready cheesy strings when you dip into it. But feel free to play with this: Adjust the amount of chile to your liking, switch the sharp cheddar to another type of cheese, add some roasted garlic, or top it with Louisiana-style hot sauce for extra kick.

The best way to serve this at a party is in a slow cooker set to low. Or else just demand everyone eat it straight out of the pot the second it's ready, while it's still piping-hot, creamy, melty perfection. **Allowing queso to go cold is a crime against Tex-Mex.**

Makes 1 large, party-size bowl of queso, about 6 cups (104 L).

1 tablespoon vegetable oil

1 cup (125 g) finely diced white onion

4 garlic cloves, minced

3 poblano peppers, roasted (see page 94), seeded, peeled, and finely diced

2 medium tomatoes, seeded and finely diced

Salt and black pepper

1 package (2 pounds/910 g) processed cheese, such as Velveeta, cut into ½-inch (12-mm) cubes

1 cup (115 g) shredded sharp cheddar cheese

1 cup (40 g) chopped fresh cilantro (optional)

Heat the oil in a medium pot over medium heat and add the onion and garlic. Sauté until soft, 3 to 5 minutes. Add the poblanos and tomatoes and a pinch of salt and black pepper. Sauté for another minute.

Turn the heat down to low. Add a handful of the processed cheese at a time, stirring between each addition until the cheese melts and the mixture is smooth. When all of the processed cheese is melted, add the sharp cheddar and stir until it has melted as well. Stir in the cilantro, if using, reserving a little bit of it to sprinkle on top as garnish. Serve immediately.

Chile con Carne Enchiladas

Cheese enchiladas doused in chile con carne sauce are **the epitome of classic Tex-Mex.** This version is made with Maudie's classic chile sauce—meaning it's pretty much just meat and chile powder. Corn tortillas are wrapped around a gooey, yellow cheese filling, and then smothered with chile sauce, chopped onions, and cilantro. This right here is proper Texas comfort food.

Restaurants don't make enchiladas quite the same way you would at home: They make them one serving at a time, directly on the plate, which is then run under a broiler-like heating element called a salamander (hence servers constantly warning you about hot plates). At home, it's easier to do them in family-size batches in a baking dish in the oven, and cook them just long enough that everything gets piping hot. Serve these with Rice and Beans (page 76).

Serves 6 with 2 enchiladas each.

1 recipe Chile con Carne Sauce (page 229), warm

¼ cup (60 ml) vegetable oil

12 corn tortillas

3 cups (340 g) shredded mild cheddar, Colby, or American cheese

Chopped onions (optional)

Chopped fresh cilantro (optional)

Heat the oven to 400°F (205°C).

Ladle about 1 cup (240 ml) of the sauce into a greased 9 by 13-inch (23 by 33-cm) baking dish.

Heat the oil in a small skillet and add a tortilla; cook until just soft, 5 seconds on each side. Remove the tortilla to a plate and place a row of shredded cheese about the thickness of your thumb down the center of the tortilla. Roll the tortilla and place it in the baking dish. Repeat this process until all of the tortillas are used and the baking dish holds a row of tightly rolled tortillas. Ladle the rest of the sauce over the top and sprinkle with any remaining cheese.

Bake until bubbling and hot, about 10 minutes, and serve, topped with chopped onions and cilantro, if desired.

Chipotle Lamb Loin Chops

Fonda San Miguel

The key to these lovely smoky lamb chops is to toast and grind your own chipotle powder. You can use store-bought if you like, but it is not super difficult to make the seasoning yourself and it makes a world of difference. This will make more of the chipotle rub than you'll need, and the leftover rub is delicious on basically anything you would cook on the grill.

Serves 6.

For the rub

¼ cup (24 g) chipotle chile powder (see instructions or use store bought)

¼ cup (60 ml) vegetable oil

3 dried chipotle chiles, seeds and stems removed

1 dried ancho chile, seeds and stems removed

6 garlic cloves, peeled

⅓ cup (80 g) salt

2 tablespoons dried Mexican oregano

For the lamb chops

4 pounds (1.8 kg) bone-in loin lamb chops

2 tablespoons olive oil

To make the chipotle powder: Heat the oil in a skillet over medium heat. Fry the chipotle and ancho chiles in batches, turning them as they puff up, about 10 seconds on each side. Drain on paper towels and let cool; the chiles should be crisp and dry once cooled. Grind into a powder in a spice grinder or, in a pinch, a food processor.

Put the chipotle powder, the garlic, salt, and oregano in a food processor and grind into a coarse rub. If the rub looks wet, dry it in a 150°F (65°C) oven for an hour or so. Let cool. The rub will keep in an airtight container in the pantry for up to three months.

Make the lamb chops: Rub the lamb chops all over with the oil. Then dust the chops with the rub, brushing off any seasoning that doesn't stick.

Heat a charcoal grill (or a cast-iron grill pan) to high heat. Grill the lamb chops for about 3 minutes on each side for medium-rare, and let rest for 5 minutes before serving.

Chayote Slaw with Chile Arbol Dressing

La Condesa

This is a colorful, spicy salad that would be at home at a cookout or served with grilled meat like Chipotle Lamb Loin Chops (page 82).

Serves 6 as a side.

2 cups (220 g) grated chayote

2 cups (220 g) grated jicama

2 Fresno chiles, cut into thin strips

½ cup (55 g) thinly sliced red onion

Arbol dressing (recipe follows)

Palm dressing (recipe follows)

¼ cup (10 g) chopped fresh cilantro

Combine the chayote, jicama, chiles, and onion in a bowl. Add the arbol dressing—watch out, it's spicy—and palm dressing to taste, then fold in the cilantro and serve.

Arbol Dressing

Yields 1 cup.

10 dried arbol chiles

⅓ cup (15 g) finely chopped fresh cilantro

⅓ cup (17 g) finely chopped fresh parsley

2 tablespoons finely chopped fresh epazote (optional)

1 tablespoon finely chopped fresh mint

½ cup (120 ml) olive oil

Grated zest and juice of 2 lemons

1 tablespoon agave nectar

Salt and black pepper to taste

Toast the chiles in a small saucepan over medium heat until they are fragrant, about 1 minute, watching carefully to make sure they don't burn. Let the chiles cool, then chop them finely.

Put the chiles in a bowl with the cilantro, parsley, epazote (if using), mint, oil, lemon zest and juice, and agave and whisk to combine. Season with salt and black pepper.

Palm Dressing

Yields ½ cup.

¼ cup (85 g) grated palm sugar

¼ cup (60 ml) fresh lime juice

Microwave the palm sugar for about 5 seconds to soften, then add the lime juice. Whisk to combine.

Mole Rojo with Chicken

El Naranjo

Much like Fonda San Miguel, El Naranjo is a restaurant that seeks to introduce Austinites to the regional specialties of Mexico. Specializing in Oaxacan food—husband-and-wife owners Iliana de la Vega and Ernesto Torrealba had a restaurant there before moving to Austin—El Naranjo is known for the complex sauces of that region, called moles.

This red mole combines chiles, cinnamon, sesame, chocolate, pecans, and more for a sauce that is velvety and deep. It's also good with turkey, or as a sauce for enchiladas.

Serves 8.

Salt

½ white onion, peeled

4 whole, unpeeled garlic cloves

2 whole chickens, cut into 8 pieces each, or 16 pieces of bone-in, skin-on chicken thighs and drumsticks

Mole rojo (recipe opposite)

Bring a large pot of salted water to a boil and add the onion and garlic. Once the water is boiling really hard, add the chicken. Immediately reduce the heat to barely a simmer and cook for 45 minutes, until the chicken pieces float on top. Remove the chicken to a platter and cover it with mole rojo.

Mole Rojo

8 ounces (225 g) dried ancho
chiles

8 ounces (225 g) dried guajillo
chiles

1 pound (455 g) Roma tomatoes

1 white onion, cut in half, peeled

6 whole, unpeeled garlic cloves

3 tablespoons vegetable oil

½ cup (50 g) pecans

½ cup (75 g) roasted unsalted
peanuts

¼ cup (40 g) brown sesame seeds

1 (1-inch/2.5-cm) stick Mexican
canela (Ceylon cinnamon)

8 black peppercorns

4 whole cloves

1 tablespoon dried Mexican
oregano

1½ cups (360 ml) chicken stock

7 ounces (200 g) Mexican chocolate, such as Abuelita

Salt

Sugar

Remove the stems, seeds, and veins
from the chiles and toast them in
a dry skillet for 10 to 15 seconds,
until fragrant. Put the chiles in a
bowl and cover with very hot water,
then let soak for 15 minutes.

Set a cast-iron pan over medium-
high heat and roast the tomatoes,
onion, and garlic until they begin to
show brown spots.

Remove from the pan and set
aside. When completely cool, peel
the garlic.

Heat 1½ tablespoons of the oil in
a skillet over medium heat and add
the pecans and peanuts. Sauté
until toasted, about 2 minutes, then
add the sesame seeds, canela,
peppercorns, cloves, and oregano
and remove from the heat.

Drain the chiles and put them in
a blender or food processor. Add
about ½ cup (120 ml) fresh water
and blend until smooth. Transfer
the chile puree to a bowl. In the
blender, combine the roasted
vegetables and the pecan mixture
with ½ cup (120 ml) water and
blend until smooth. If the chile or
vegetable mixture seems very gritty,
pass it through a mesh strainer.

Heat the remaining 1½ tablespoons oil in a large Dutch oven
over medium heat. Add the chile
puree and fry, stirring, for about 5
minutes. Add the vegetable puree
and cook for another 5 minutes.
Add the stock and chocolate and
let the mixture simmer, stirring
occasionally, until the mole coats
the back of a spoon, about 5
minutes. Season with salt and, if
the mixture is at all bitter, sugar.

Enchiladas Tejanas

Jack Allen's Kitchen

There are probably dozens of family restaurants in Austin that serve tacos, burgers, fancy margaritas, and the like. But there is only one Jack Allen's Kitchen, where they get their ingredients from local farms, switch up the menu with the seasons, and, oh yeah, the food is incredibly good. Founded by veteran Austin chef Jack Gilmore (father of Barley Swine/Odd Duck's Bryce Gilmore), JAK is a restaurant of giant booths, killer cocktails, and daily market specials, including these fabulous enchiladas.

These are not rolled like your typical Texas-style enchiladas, although the flavors are about as Texan as it gets. Instead, they're stacked, like a lasagna, with layers of spicy, creamy tomato-based sauce and pulled chicken between the tortillas . . . and baked with eggs on top. They make a (very) hearty brunch or dinner.

Serves 6.

For the sauce

1½ cups (360 ml) JAK's Salsa
(page 221)

1½ cups (360 ml) heavy cream

For the enchiladas

2 tablespoons vegetable oil

12 corn tortillas

1 recipe Chicken Tinga (page 57)

1 cup (115 g) shredded Oaxacan
cheese or Monterey Jack

6 eggs (optional)

Heat the oven to 500°F (260°C).

Make the sauce: Combine the salsa and cream in a saucepan and simmer until slightly thickened, about 10 minutes. Remove from the heat.

Make the enchiladas: To achieve the ideal tortilla texture, heat the oil in a small sauté pan and fry the tortillas one at a time until slightly softened, 10 to 15 seconds on each side.

Grease a 9 by 13-inch (23 by 33-cm) baking dish, then spread a large spoonful of the sauce in the dish. Layer the enchiladas like you would a lasagna—flat, not rolled—in this order: tortillas, chicken, sauce. Repeat until the ingredients are used up, ending with the sauce, then sprinkle the top with the cheese.

Crack the eggs on top and bake for about 8 minutes, until the whites are set but the yolks are still runny. (Or, if not using the eggs, until the cheese is melted and the sauce is bubbly.) Let sit for 5 minutes before eating.

Butternut and Goat Cheese Chile Relleno

Alcomar

Alcomar is primarily a mariscos (seafood) restaurant, but one of its signature dishes is actually vegetarian. This makes for a showstopper of a dinner party dish: the squash, goat cheese, and chard-stuffed chiles lined up on a platter with a luxurious pistachio cream sauce ladled over them is a photo-worthy centerpiece. You can even make and stuff the chiles ahead of time, heating them when your guests arrive. The filling here also works well as a stuffing for vegetarian enchiladas (see page 80).

Serves 8.

4 cups (560 g) peeled, seeded, and ½-inch (12-mm) diced butternut squash (about 1 medium)

4 tablespoons (60 ml) olive oil

Salt and black pepper

8 poblano peppers, as long as you can find

½ white onion, finely diced

4 garlic cloves, minced

4 cups (120 g) chopped Swiss chard leaves (ribs removed; about 1 bunch)

1 teaspoon brown sugar

8 ounces (225 g) goat cheese

1 recipe pistachio cream sauce (recipe follows), warm

¼ cup (30 g) shelled pistachios, toasted

¼ cup (45 g) pomegranate arils

Heat the oven to 400°F (205°C). Line a sheet pan with foil or parchment paper.

In a large mixing bowl, toss the squash with 1 tablespoon of the oil until coated. Season with a couple big pinches of salt and pepper. Spread the squash in a single layer on the sheet pan and roast it until cooked through but not mushy, about 20 minutes.

Roast the poblanos (see page 94) and remove their skin. Cut a slit in the chiles in order to remove the seeds, but otherwise leave them whole so you can stuff them. Set aside.

RECIPE CONTINUES ⟶

Heat a large skillet over medium-high heat. Add the remaining 3 tablespoons oil and the onion and garlic and sauté until the onion is translucent, 3 to 5 minutes. Add the Swiss chard and sauté until it wilts, about 2 minutes. Add the squash and brown sugar and season everything to taste with salt and pepper. Cook, stirring constantly, until almost all of the liquid has evaporated. Remove from the heat and let cool.

Stuff each chile half-full with the chard and squash mixture, then add 1 ounce (28 g) of the goat cheese to the middle of each pepper. Fill the chile the rest of the way with the chard and squash mixture. Place the stuffed chiles in a greased 9 by 13-inch (23 by 33-cm) baking dish. (You can make the recipe up to this point and refrigerate it, covered, as long as overnight if necessary.)

Heat the oven to 350°F (175°C). Cook the stuffed chiles until they begin to steam, about 20 minutes. (Add another 10 minutes if they are still chilled from being refrigerated.) Ladle about ½ cup (120 ml) of the pistachio sauce over the top of each chile, either on individual plates or all together on a serving plate. Sprinkle the chiles with pistachios and pomegranate seeds. Serve any leftover sauce on the side.

Pistachio Cream Sauce

3 tablespoons unsalted butter

2 tablespoons minced garlic

¼ teaspoon ground cloves

½ teaspoon ground cinnamon

Juice and grated zest of 1 lemon

½ cup (120 ml) dry white wine

1½ cups (360 ml) heavy cream

¾ cup (95 g) shelled roasted pistachios

1 teaspoon salt

1 cup (240 ml) crema or crème fraîche

Melt the butter in a saucepan over medium heat. Add the garlic and cook until golden, about 3 minutes. Add the cloves, cinnamon, lemon juice, and wine, stir, and bring to a boil. Cook to reduce the sauce until the liquid has almost completely evaporated.

Lower the heat to medium-low and add the cream. Bring to a simmer and add the lemon zest, pistachios, and salt. Let simmer for a few minutes to soften the pistachios. Remove from the heat and carefully transfer to a blender (or use an immersion blender). Blend until smooth. Pour the sauce back into the pot and bring it back to a simmer. Whisk in the crema. Taste for seasoning and serve immediately.

Cochinita Pibil

Curra's Grill

The sign at Curra's Grill says the restaurant is "All-Mex." As in Tex-Mex and interior Mexican, all rolled into one. This cochinita pibil veers toward the latter: the pork is marinated in a spicy-sweet citrus and achiote mixture, and it is then wrapped in banana leaves and cooked low and slow for a few hours. Serve these with hot fresh tortillas and chopped red onions.

Serves 12.

1 large can (7 ounces/199 g) chipotle peppers in adobo sauce, chiles minced, with the sauce

1 package (3½ ounces/100 g) achiote paste (annatto)

1 tablespoon paprika

1 cup (240 ml) orange juice

1 teaspoon ground cumin

1 teaspoon black pepper

2 teaspoons dried oregano

2 teaspoons salt

1 tablespoon chicken base or bouillon powder

1 teaspoon granulated garlic powder

1 pork shoulder (10 pounds/4.5 kg), cut into 3-inch (7.5-cm) cubes

1 cinnamon stick

2 pieces star anise

1 bay leaf

Banana leaves

In a small bowl, combine the chipotles and their sauce, the achiote, paprika, orange juice, cumin, black pepper, oregano, salt, chicken base, and garlic powder to make the marinade. Place the pork pieces in a large bowl and add the marinade as well as the cinnamon stick, star anise, and bay leaf. Stir to combine, making sure all of the pork is coated in the marinade. Cover and refrigerate overnight, or up to 24 hours.

Heat the oven to 300°F (150°C).

Line a large Dutch oven or heavy, oven-safe pot with aluminum foil, leaving plenty of excess foil hanging over the sides. Run the banana leaves under hot water to make them pliable, and then line the aluminum foil with banana leaves. Add the meat and its marinade to the banana leaf–lined pot, then cover the meat with more banana leaves, and use the foil to seal everything into a packet. (The idea is to trap the steam coming off the meat as it cooks.) Put the lid on the pot, over the foil packet.

Transfer to the oven and bake until the meat is tender, about 5 hours. Allow everything to cool for about 20 minutes before opening the banana leaf packet so you don't get burned by the steam. Pull the meat into large pieces before serving in tacos or, as they do at the restaurant, with fried plantains.

HOW TO
ROAST & PEEL
CHILES

Many recipes in this book begin with roasting chiles of all kinds, with poblanos and New Mexico green chiles (Hatch chiles) being most common. Here's how:

Wash and dry your chiles.

Ideally, roast the chiles on a grill or directly on the gas burners on your stove (not in a pan, but directly on the grates). Turn the chiles periodically with tongs until the skin is blistered all over—don't worry if the skin burns, but if the chile catches fire you've gone too far. If you have an electric stovetop, you can roast the chiles on a foil-lined baking sheet in the oven at 400°F (205°C) for about 10 minutes, or until the skin blisters. (The oven method is also good if you need to process a lot of chiles in a short amount of time.) You can also broil the chiles on a foil-lined baking sheet until blistered, flipping them with tongs halfway through in order to blister both sides.

When the chiles are fully blistered and piping hot, put them in a plastic bag or a heat-tolerant glass bowl covered with a pot lid or plate. This allows the chiles to steam themselves with their own heat, loosening the skin further. Let them cool completely in the bag or bowl, or at least until you can easily handle them, about 20 minutes.

Refer to your recipe, but in general, remove the skin, seeds, stem, and veins from the chiles and dispose of them. You might want to wear disposable gloves for this step, especially if you have sensitive skin, or use a butter knife to scrape away the charred skin. You should now have chile flesh that's ready to be used in whatever recipe you're making.

CHAPTER 4

TEXAS STANDARDS

Capital of
Texas Cooking

People who don't know better have, upon occasion, claimed that Austin's not "real" Texas, thanks to its hipster reputation and liberal leanings that seem to contrast with the rest of the state. But when it comes to food, Austin can be best described as a concentrated version of Texas. The university, the state capital, and, more recently, the tech industry have brought people here from all over the state. Not to mention a history of transplants from all over the US (and the rest of the world).

Accordingly, you can find many Texan and broader southern specialties in Austin. Dishes like chicken fried steak and mac 'n' cheese, as well as Gulf seafood preparations like baked oysters, can be found throughout the city. These culinary traditions represent the ways in which Texas, for all its independent streak, is often very much a part of the broader American South. Or at least it is when it comes to food.

True to Austin's sensibilities, restaurants here put their own spin on the classics. The result is jalapeño-laced meatloaf served with barbecue sauce, secret-ingredient fried chicken, and an okra dish that will convert even the most ardent haters.

Not to mention a steak dinner to end all steak dinners. Texas is cattle country, after all.

Chicken Fried Steak with Cream Gravy

The Broken Spoke

A sign outside the Broken Spoke says they have the "best chicken fried steak in town," which may be true. They are, however, infinitely better known for being one of the greatest honky-tonks in the world. Founded in 1964, the Broken Spoke is the best place in Austin to go two-stepping (don't worry, they give lessons) and has hosted such luminaries as Bob Wills & His Texas Playboys, Willie Nelson, George Strait, and more.

If you eat this dish while listening to old-timey western swing, it will taste like pure Texas. I promise.

Serves 6.

1 egg

1 cup (240 ml) buttermilk

1 tablespoon salt

1 tablespoon black pepper

1 cup (125 g) all-purpose flour, plus ¼ cup (30 g) for the gravy

1 cup (90 g) cracker meal (or crushed saltines)

6 cube steaks (3 ounces/85 g each), or pieces of top sirloin pounded out with a meat tenderizer

Vegetable oil for frying

2 cups (480 ml) whole milk

Whisk together the egg, buttermilk, salt, and pepper in a mixing bowl.

Combine the 1 cup (125 g) flour and cracker meal in a shallow bowl. One at a time, double-bread the steaks: dip each steak in the flour mixture, patting it onto the sides. Submerge the steak in the egg mixture, then dip it into the flour again.

Pour ½ inch (12 mm) oil into a large skillet and heat over medium-high heat until hot but not smoking. Fry the steaks; you may have to work in batches so as not to crowd the pan. Cook the steaks until the batter is golden, about 3 minutes per side. Set the steaks on paper towels to drain and rest for about 5 minutes.

While the steaks rest, make the gravy: Pour all but about ¼ cup (60 ml) oil out of the frying pan. Reduce the heat to medium and add ¼ cup (30 g) flour to the skillet, using a whisk to combine it with any leftover grease and drippings from the steaks. Add the milk and cook, stirring, until the mixture is smooth and thickens to a gravy consistency. Season with salt and pepper and serve over the steaks.

Pimento Cheese

Noble Sandwich Co.

Pimento cheese, a spread made from shredded cheddar, red peppers, and mayonnaise, has seen a revival in recent years. This version, from Noble Sandwich Co., calls for you to roast your own bell peppers instead of using traditional canned pimentos. The fresh flavor is worth the bit of extra effort. Serve this with chips or crackers or raw vegetables, or on sandwiches (which is, of course, how Noble serves them).

Makes 1½ quarts (1.4 L) of pimento cheese, a decent-size bowl for a party.

3 red bell peppers

1½ pounds (680 g) shredded sharp cheddar cheese

1 cup (240 ml) mayonnaise

2 teaspoons Worcestershire sauce

1 tablespoon sriracha

3 scallions, thinly sliced

1 teaspoon black pepper

1 teaspoon roasted garlic powder

2 teaspoons paprika

1 tablespoon apple cider vinegar

Salt to taste

Roast the bell peppers (see page 94) and, once they've cooled, remove the skin, seeds, and stems (it's okay to leave a little bit of charred skin, but try to get most of it off). Pulse the peppers in a food processor until finely chopped but not pureed.

Put the peppers along with the remaining ingredients in the bowl of a stand mixer and mix until thoroughly combined. Serve immediately or store, covered, in the refrigerator for up to 3 days.

A MCGUIRE MOORMAN STEAK DINNER

Restauranting duo Larry McGuire and Tom Moorman were in their early twenties when they opened their first restaurant, Lamberts, in 2006. Since then, they've opened several additional restaurants and become known for meticulously designed spaces and elegant food. Over the past decade, their restaurants helped shape what people have come to expect in Austin dining: a vibrant, stylish, and laid-back atmosphere with phenomenal food and a killer soundtrack.

The following recipes are from three different McGuire Moorman Hospitality restaurants: Lamberts (upscale barbecue), Clark's (seafood), and Jeffrey's (MMH's refresh of a landmark Austin steakhouse). Here, these dishes are brought together as a traditional steakhouse dinner—steak, greens, and mashed potatoes—but given a bit of that McGuire Moorman flair.

Mustard and Brown Sugar–Crusted Ribeye

Lamberts

This ribeye from Lamberts is a bit more dressed up than your standard grilled ribeye, with an assist from whole-grain mustard butter and a crispy brown sugar crust for truly spectacular flavor. Roasted garlic is served on the side as a condiment—you can spread a little on each bite of steak, or mix it in with the Pommes Puree (page 106), or spread it on bread.

Serves 2.

1 ribeye steak (18 ounces/510 g)

1 teaspoon olive oil

Salt and black pepper

Whole-grain mustard butter (recipe follows)

2 tablespoons dark brown sugar

Whole roasted garlic (recipe opposite)

Prepare a hot grill. Rub the steak with the oil, then season it lightly with salt and pepper. Grill the steak to your desired level of doneness, 3 to 4 minutes on each side for medium-rare (if it's an especially thick steak, it could need longer). Remove from the heat and let the steak rest for 8 to 10 minutes.

Meanwhile, heat the broiler. Spread a thin layer of mustard butter evenly all over the ribeye, and sprinkle it on both sides with the brown sugar. Broil the steak just until the brown sugar is caramelized, about 1 minute on each side, depending on how mighty your broiler is. Slice the steak against the grain and serve with the roasted garlic on the side.

Whole-Grain Mustard Butter

4 tablespoons (55 g) unsalted butter, softened

½ tablespoon Dijon mustard

2 teaspoons whole-grain mustard

¼ teaspoon sugar

Salt and black pepper to taste

In a bowl, whisk all the ingredients together until combined. Set aside while preparing the steak.

Whole Roasted Garlic

1 head of garlic

1 tablespoon olive oil

Salt and black pepper

Heat the oven to 300°F (150°C).

Cut off the top off of the garlic, exposing the cloves. Drizzle the cloves with olive oil, then season lightly with salt and pepper. Wrap the head of garlic in a piece of foil; add 1 tablespoon water before sealing the foil packet.

Roast the garlic for about 1 hour, or until fully cooked and soft. You'll want to serve it warm, but let it cool slightly before opening the foil packet so you don't burn yourself on the steam.

HOT HOT HOT
A NOTE ON COOKING IN THE HEAT

It gets hot in Texas. Really, really, unbearably, terribly hot. And while it makes for great swimming weather, it can seriously hinder those of us who like to cook.

Bless the toaster oven, your greatest ally during the endless summer. During the hot months, I use my toaster oven for everything I'd normally cook in a full-size oven, from chicken thighs to enchiladas. A toaster oven makes this steak a great hot-weather recipe: you can roast the garlic in the toaster oven, grill the steak outside, and then bring it inside to broil in—you guessed it—the toaster oven. All without heating up your house. (Your air-conditioning bill will thank you.)

Pommes Puree

Jeffrey's

Jeffrey's opened in Clarksville in 1975, and for decades it has been the steakhouse of choice for visiting big shots and locals celebrating anniversaries and birthdays. McGuire Moorman Hospitality took over the space in 2013 and gave the restaurant a makeover for the ages. Jeffrey's remains a steakhouse, but one with modern vision and design (and martini carts).

That said, this recipe is about as old-school as it gets: mashed potatoes with as much cream and butter as they can hold. Sure, it's decadent and over the top, but hey, that's what a steak dinner's all about.

Serves 6.

4 pounds (1.8 kg) Yukon gold potatoes, peeled and diced

1 tablespoon kosher salt, plus more to taste

2 cups (480 ml) heavy cream

½ cup (1 stick/115 g) unsalted butter

Heat the oven to 300°F (150°C).

In a large pot, cover the potatoes with water and add 1 tablespoon salt. Bring to a boil, then reduce the heat to a simmer. Simmer until the potatoes are cooked through, about 20 minutes.

Drain the potatoes well, and then spread them on a sheet pan in a single layer. Dry them in the oven for about 3 minutes.

While the potatoes are drying in the oven, heat the cream and butter together in a small saucepan until the butter is melted. Run the potatoes through a food mill or potato ricer into a pot or mixing bowl, and then add the hot cream and butter. You'll have to stir it quite a bit to incorporate the dairy, but in the end you should have a smooth, silky puree. Season to taste with salt and serve.

Grilled Tuscan Kale

Clark's

To round out the steak dinner, some greens from Clark's. This works best with lacinato kale, but use whatever type of kale is available and looks good. The greens are grilled just briefly—you can use the last of the coal embers while the steak rests, if you're making the whole steak dinner—and then tossed with lemon juice and pine nuts for a smoky and bright vegetable side.

Serves 4 to 6.

1 bunch kale, stems removed, leaves left whole

3 tablespoons olive oil

Pinch of red chile flakes

Salt and black pepper

Juice and grated zest of ½ lemon

¼ cup (25 g) freshly grated Parmesan cheese

2 tablespoons pine nuts, toasted

In a large mixing bowl, drizzle the kale with 2 tablespoons of the oil. Season with chile flakes, salt, and black pepper, and toss together until everything is covered with seasoning.

Prepare a hot grill (or heat a grill pan over high heat on the stovetop). Grill the kale directly on the grates in one large bunch, turning periodically with tongs until it is cooked and tender, about 4 minutes.

Transfer the kale to a mixing bowl and add the lemon juice and the remaining 1 tablespoon oil. Toss to combine, then transfer the dressed kale to a serving dish. Finish by sprinkling the greens with the cheese, lemon zest, and pine nuts.

Note: If you have delicate, early-season kale, you can leave the stems on.

Lucy's Fried Chicken

Lucy's Fried Chicken

Chef James Holmes's grandmother Lucy must have been one incredible woman, as she inspired Holmes to name both his daughter and his restaurants after her. One thing's for sure: she had a fantastic fried chicken recipe. And while Holmes didn't divulge the exact secret to Lucy's seasoning mix, he says this will get you pretty close.

Lucy's uses their house-made Bayou Betty hot sauce for this recipe, but Holmes says "go with your favorite. Or, for the faint of heart, you may omit." Either way, he recommends drinking Lone Star beer both while you prepare the chicken* and while you eat it, and that you eat the leftovers cold the next day.

*Please be careful when frying!

Serves 4 to 6.

1 quart (960 ml) buttermilk

½ cup (120 ml) Louisiana-style hot sauce

2 tablespoons soy sauce

2 small fryer chickens (about 2 pounds/910 g each), cut into 10 pieces each (with the breast split), or have the butcher cut them for you

6 cups (770 g) all-purpose flour

¼ cup (60 g) salt

¼ cup (28 g) black pepper

1 tablespoon granulated garlic powder

1 tablespoon onion powder

1 tablespoon ground cayenne

1 gallon (3.78 L) peanut oil

In a large bowl, stir together the buttermilk, hot sauce, and soy sauce. Add the chicken and let it marinate in the refrigerator for at least 12 hours, but ideally 48 hours.

When it's time to fry, mix together the flour, salt, black pepper, garlic powder, onion powder, and cayenne in a large, shallow dish. Heat the oil in a large, deep pot to 325°F (165°C).

While the oil heats up, coat the chicken: Take each piece out of the marinade and dip it in the flour mixture, massaging the seasoning into the chicken. (Holmes says this is the key to achieving that crispy crust.) As you coat the chicken, separate the pieces into two groups: dark meat (thighs and wings) and white meat (breasts). It will be harder to tell which is which once they're covered in batter.

Fry the chicken in batches according to the type of meat: dark meat fries with dark meat, white meat fries with white meat. Don't crowd the pot; you should only have one layer of meat frying at a time. Fry the chicken until the crust is golden brown all over, 10 to 12 minutes per batch. Transfer the fried chicken to a baking sheet lined with paper towels while you fry the rest. Serve either hot or cold.

Parkside Macaroni

Parkside

Parkside is Austin chef and restaurateur Shawn Cirkiel's flagship restaurant. Opened in 2008, Parkside serves its twist on classic Americana, like its signature macaroni and cheese. The beauty of this dish? It would be as at home on your grandmother's Thanksgiving buffet as it would be in a white-tablecloth restaurant.

Serves 8.

1 pound (455 g) dried elbow macaroni

Salt

4 tablespoons (55 g) unsalted butter

½ cup (65 g) finely chopped yellow onion

¼ cup (30 g) all-purpose flour

4 cups (960 ml) whole milk, cold

1 bay leaf

3 black peppercorns

2 sprigs fresh thyme

2 cups (215 g) shredded Gruyère cheese

2 cups (225 g) shredded white cheddar cheese

½ cup (25 g) dried bread crumbs

¼ cup (25 g) shredded Parmesan cheese

Ground black pepper

Heat the oven to 400°F (205°C).

Boil the pasta in salted water until slightly undercooked, about 2 minutes less than the package's instructions say to cook it. Drain and set aside.

Melt the butter in a saucepan over medium heat. Add the onion and cook until it is translucent, about 3 minutes. Turn the heat to low and add the flour; cook for 2 minutes, stirring constantly. Gradually whisk in the cold milk, then add the bay leaf, peppercorns, and thyme. Bring the sauce back to a simmer and simmer until slightly thickened, about 5 minutes.

Strain the sauce into a medium pot. Set the pot over low heat and gradually stir in the Gruyère and cheddar, whisking until smooth. Season to taste with salt and ground pepper. Add the cooked pasta and stir to combine, making sure the sauce is evenly distributed through the pasta.

In a small bowl, combine the bread crumbs and Parmesan.

Pour the pasta into a greased 9 by 13-inch (23 by 33-cm) baking dish and top with the bread crumb mixture. Bake until the sides are bubbling and the top is golden brown, about 20 minutes.

Welcome to the Neon Jungle

Evan Voyles has been designing and building neon signs for Austin stores and restaurants at his studio, The Neon Jungle, since 1994. His work includes many iconic Austin images, including signs at the original Alamo Drafthouse, Magnolia Cafe, Lucy's Fried Chicken, and much of the neon on the South Congress shopping strip. Here he explains how these signs became the signature for so many businesses and came to encapsulate the aesthetic of Austin itself.

When my antiques store burned down in 1994, I had a bunch of signs out back in what I called the neon jungle. They weren't harmed by the fire. Everything inside was gone, cooked. I had a pair of jeans, a pair of boots, and about twenty killer American neon signs in back. I was in the sign business overnight.

It started out along South Congress, and South Congress is my biggest body of work today. I tried to build a community of signs to go with the community of neighbors. I've spent twenty years trying to carefully craft a chess set along that row. I made South Congress look that way, and I'm very proud to have contributed to the visual culture of my hometown.

What attracted me to signs in the first place is that you've basically got three types of artwork in front of you. You've got sculpture, you've got painting, and then the neon is line-drawing with light. Ideally these all work with each other instead of against each other. We don't live in a world that's all night and we don't live in a world that's all day. During the day, the sculpture and the painting make the point. Neon in broad sunlight—you can't see it. It might as well not be there.

I figured the signs would last if I built them like the old guys did. I was collecting signs that were sixty, seventy years old, and they still worked. I thought, "If I just do it like these guys, my work will stand for decades." My signs look handmade because they are handmade. Flawless isn't my taste. I want the signs to look funky. I'm channeling the '30s and the '40s, when things were made to the best of their abilities, with the best of the materials they had.

I rivet everything, and now I'm almost making a fetish out of it. The rivets aren't decorative—they hold it together. They're structurally necessary. Nobody uses rivets anymore. Welding is faster, and people think welding looks better. I don't. I am ruled by the old methods.

A sign also needs delight. Delight is the sugar, delight is the salt, delight is the hook that gets you in. It's one thing to look at a sign and go, "Yeah, okay. It says that." It's another to look at a sign and go, "Oh man, I want to go there."

It isn't just how the piece works for me or the client, it's how the piece works in the context of where the sun is, where the trees are, where the traffic's coming from, where the wind is coming from, how fast you're going, how far up the building it is, where the driveway cuts, where the door is, what are your hours, what are you selling?

Take Justine's. That restaurant was on the edge of town when it opened. The East Side was not hip. Who knew East Fifth went that far? Who even knew there were houses over there? I'd tell people, "Here's the thing, go at night because they're not open during the day, and at the end of a very long, dark tunnel you're going to see a flickering light underneath those trees."

That's the sign—the trees catch it. The whole restaurant glows; it's this bright spot in the night. Is that not what we all want, the bright spot in the night?

Blackened Drum with Shrimp Cream Sauce

Quality Seafood

Quality Seafood has been in business, in one form or another, since 1938. It currently occupies a large storefront on Airport Boulevard, and it includes a seafood market, oyster bar, and restaurant. The market is one of the best places in town to source Gulf seafood, and, as this creamy, decadent blackened drum dish shows, they also know what to do with it.

You can buy store-bought blackening spice or make your own—either way works.

Serves 2.

2 fillets red or black drum
(6 to 8 ounces/170 to 225 g each)

3 tablespoons blackening spice,
store-bought or homemade
(recipe follows)

3 tablespoons unsalted butter

Shrimp cream sauce (recipe follows)

Pat the fillets dry and press the spice mix onto the surface. Brush off any seasoning that doesn't stick to the fish. (If you're using store-bought blackening seasoning, have a light hand with it, as these tend to be saltier than homemade.)

Heat a cast-iron skillet over high heat until hot but not smoking. Melt the butter in the pan and add the fish. Cook on each side until the fillets turn white on the edges (about 2 minutes per side). Remove the fish and serve with shrimp cream sauce.

Shrimp Cream Sauce

1 tablespoon olive oil

1 tablespoon minced shallot

1 garlic clove, minced

8 ounces (225 g) Texas Brown shrimp, peeled and deveined, chopped

1 teaspoon Creole seasoning

1 cup (240 ml) heavy cream

½ tablespoon Tabasco sauce

½ tablespoon Worcestershire sauce

½ tablespoon unsalted butter

Salt and black pepper

2 tablespoons chopped scallion

Heat the oil in a sauté pan over medium heat. Add the shallot and garlic and sauté for 30 seconds, then add the shrimp and Creole seasoning. Sauté for 1 to 2 minutes. Add the cream, hot sauce, and Worcestershire sauce. Bring to a boil, then reduce the heat to a simmer. Simmer the sauce until it thickens and reduces by half, about 5 minutes. Add the butter, season with salt and pepper, and fold in the scallion. Serve hot.

Homemade Blackening Spice

1 tablespoon paprika

2 teaspoons granulated garlic powder

2 teaspoons chili powder

1 teaspoon salt

1 teaspoon black pepper

1 teaspoon dried thyme

½ teaspoon ground cayenne

½ teaspoon ground cumin

Combine the paprika, garlic powder, chili powder, salt, black pepper, thyme, cayenne, and cumin together in a small bowl.

Baked Oysters

Mongers Market + Kitchen

Gulf oysters are often quite large, and while they're plenty good raw, their size lends them nicely to baked or grilled preparations. You'll find baked oysters all over the Gulf Coast, particularly in New Orleans, but the tradition has crept all the way up to Austin in these baked oysters from Mongers, a restaurant and fish market that specializes in Gulf seafood. This recipe also works well on the grill, if you like your oysters a little bit smoky.

Serves 6.

2 cups (480 ml) milk

1 shallot, cut in half, peeled

1 bay leaf

2 whole cloves

3 tablespoons unsalted butter, melted

3 tablespoons flour

Salt and white pepper

Pinch of grated nutmeg

1 ounce (28 g) Gruyère cheese, grated

1 ounce (28 g) Parmesan cheese, grated

1 tablespoon chopped fresh tarragon

1 tablespoon chopped fresh chives

24 to 30 Gulf oysters, scrubbed and shucked on the half shell

⅓ cup (35 g) toasted bread crumbs

Heat the oven to 400°F (205°C).

In a medium saucepan, heat the milk, shallot, bay leaf, and cloves until the mixture simmers. Remove from the heat and let the milk steep for 30 minutes.

Put the butter and flour in a skillet over medium heat. Whisk the mixture constantly until the flour no longer has a raw taste, about 2 minutes. Remove from the heat and set aside.

Remove the shallot, bay leaf, and cloves from the milk and return the milk to a simmer over low heat. Add the flour mixture to the milk and whisk until smooth. Cook the sauce, whisking often, for 10 to 15 more minutes, until thickened. Season with salt, white pepper, and nutmeg.

Remove the sauce from the heat and add the cheeses and herbs, stirring until the cheese is melted. Let cool to room temperature.

Top each oyster with 1 tablespoon sauce and bake on a sheet pan for 15 minutes, until the sauce is browned and bubbling. Top with bread crumbs and serve.

Meatloaf

Jacoby's Meat and Mercantile

Here's Jacoby's take on meatloaf, which gets a hint of Texas flavor from jalapeños and barbecue sauce. This is one of the juiciest meat-loaves I've ever made, which is to say that it throws off a lot of liquid while cooking (heed the advice to cook it on a rimmed sheet pan) and is also astoundingly delicious.

Serves 6 to 8 with leftovers for sandwiches.

2 tablespoons vegetable oil

⅔ cup (85 g) finely diced onion

⅓ cup (50 g) finely diced jalapeños

3 eggs

⅔ cup (55 g) panko bread crumbs

2 teaspoons salt

1 teaspoon black pepper

⅓ cup (75 ml) chicken stock

2 teaspoons minced fresh rosemary

2 teaspoons minced fresh thyme

3 pounds (1.4 kg) ground beef (80/20)

Barbecue sauce (recipe follows)

Heat the oven to 375°F (190°C).

Heat the vegetable oil in a sauté pan. Add the onion and jalapeños and cook until the onion is translucent, 3 to 5 minutes. Remove from the heat and set aside to cool.

Once the cooked vegetables have cooled, combine them with the eggs, panko, salt, pepper, stock, rosemary, and thyme in a medium bowl and stir until combined.

Add the wet mixture to the beef in a large mixing bowl and mix with your (very clean!) hands until well incorporated.

Form the meatloaf by forcefully throwing small handfuls of the meat mixture into a loaf pan, about ¼ cup (60 ml) at a time. (This step may seem like an odd thing to do, but it will help the meatloaf develop a nice texture.) Press the meat down so the mixture is evenly pressed into the pan and forms a nice loaf shape.

Cover the loaf pan with foil and set it on a sheet pan, in order to catch any drippings that might bubble out during cooking. Bake the meatloaf for 40 minutes, then remove the foil and bake for 25 more minutes or until it reaches an internal temperature of 150°F (66°C).

Remove the meatloaf from the oven and allow it to cool in the pan for 15 to 20 minutes. The meatloaf will shrink slightly during baking, and it throws off quite a bit of liquid.

Remove the loaf from the pan, leaving the liquid behind, and serve it in thick slices with barbecue sauce.

Barbecue Sauce

¼ cup (60 ml) corn syrup

¼ cup (60 ml) molasses

⅓ cup (75 ml) apple cider vinegar

⅓ cup (75 ml) ketchup

1 tablespoon homemade blackening spice (page 115)

Combine all the ingredients in a saucepan and bring just to a boil. Immediately remove from the heat and serve warm.

Okra with Walnuts

Contigo

Contigo is a restaurant you would only find in Austin. The restaurant is almost entirely outdoors, a patio of long tables and picnic benches, trussed with strings of lights. Chef Andrew Wiseheart and his team prepare dressed-up bar food with a Texas accent, including rabbit and dumplings, crispy fried green beans, and one of the city's finest burgers.

This, though, might just be my favorite thing on the menu. Okra and walnuts are a brilliant pairing, as the seeds of the okra mimic the texture of the walnuts. Jalapeño and vinegar give it welcome sass. Okra haters, try this one. You might surprise yourselves.

Serves 6 as a side.

3 tablespoons vegetable oil

1 pound (455 g) okra, sliced ½ inch (12 mm) thick on a bias

½ teaspoon salt, plus more to taste

½ cup (60 g) thinly sliced shallot

1 jalapeño, thinly sliced

4 garlic cloves, thinly sliced

½ cup (50 g) toasted walnuts, roughly chopped

½ cup (75 g) Sun Gold, Juliet, or cherry tomatoes, cut in half

½ cup (120 ml) sherry vinegar

4 tablespoons (115 g) cold butter

Black pepper

Heat the oil in a large sauté pan or cast-iron skillet until nearly smoking. Add the okra and ½ teaspoon salt and sauté until it begins to brown, about 1 minute.

Add the shallot and jalapeño and sauté until the shallot softens, about 1 minute. Add the garlic and sauté for 30 seconds. Add the walnuts, tomatoes, and vinegar; cook until almost of the vinegar has evaporated.

Remove from the heat, add the butter, and toss until it is melted and the vegetables are glazed. Serve immediately.

CHAPTER 5

NEW
AUSTIN
CLASSICS

Once upon a time, Austin was a place to get Tex-Mex, barbecue, and hippie college student vegetarian food. And not much else. But, as anyone here will tell you, the city has changed. Austin keeps getting bigger, and along with the city's growth, there's been a restaurant RENAISSANCE.

Arguably, Austin's modern restaurant era started with Uchi. Not only did chef Tyson Cole upend expectations of the type of food diners could get in Austin when he opened his sushi restaurant in 2003, he laid the foundation for Austin chefs to move beyond the constraints of Central Texas foodways. Some of the best chefs in Austin have gone through Uchi's kitchen, including Paul Qui (East Side King, Kuneho), Nicholas Yanes (Juniper), and Takehiro Asazu (Kome)—and none of them is cooking what's typically thought of as Texan cuisine.

Another factor that had a major impact on Austin's growing restaurant scene was the post-recession food truck BOOM that began in 2009. Many of the best restaurants in Austin began as food trucks, including East Side King, the massively popular Detroit-style pizzeria Via 313, and Bryce Gilmore's Odd Duck Farm to Trailer. Gilmore, in fact, got a *Food & Wine* Best New Chef nod based on the sophisticated food he managed to knock out of his tiny red trailer. A small painting of the original truck hangs in the current space—a building too glassy and bright to be called a brick-and-mortar.

This chapter includes recipes from Lenoir, Chef Todd Duplechan's nod to hot-weather cuisine and the bounty of Central Texas; Sway, a stylish Thai restaurant from the folks behind La Condesa; Bufalina, amazing Neapolitan-style pizza; Emmer & Rye, an innovative restaurant that explores the wide world of grains; and the Whip-In, a convenience store–turned–brewpub that incorporates Indian flavors. And this is just a sampling of the evolving Austin restaurant landscape—new entries open seemingly every day.

Note: This chapter contains the most fine-dining restaurants of any chapter in this book, which also means it contains the most technically difficult recipes. Feel free to make all or part of the recipes according to your ability—some of the subrecipes are amazing on their own.

Uchiviche

Uchi

This dish is classic Uchi: packed with flavor and bursting with acidity, a perfect showcase for fish. Accordingly, make sure you use the highest quality, freshest fish you can get your hands on.

Serves 4 as an appetizer, but easily doubles to make a great dish for a cocktail party.

¼ teaspoon sugar

½ tablespoon hot water

½ tablespoon rice vinegar

1 teaspoon soy sauce

1 teaspoon distilled white vinegar

½ teaspoon fresh yuzu juice (or lime juice if you can't find yuzu)

½ orange bell pepper, sliced into thin strips

4 cherry tomatoes, cut in half

½ Thai chile pepper, sliced extra thin

10 fresh cilantro leaves

2 ounces (55 g) whitefish (striped bass or red snapper), cut into ½-inch (12-mm) cubes

2 ounces (55 g) king salmon, cut into ½-inch (12-mm) cubes

½ garlic clove, grated

Salt and black pepper

1 ounce (28 g/one large handful) arugula

Chill a stainless-steel bowl and a serving plate in the refrigerator for at least 20 minutes.

In a small bowl, combine the sugar with hot water to dissolve, then add the rice vinegar, soy sauce, white vinegar, and yuzu juice. Set the sauce aside.

In the chilled bowl, mix together the bell pepper, tomatoes, chile, cilantro, whitefish, salmon, and garlic. Season with salt and pepper. Add the sauce, tossing everything together to combine. Place on the chilled plate and sprinkle the arugula on top.

Beet Fries

East Side King

These are iconic. The original East Side King food truck behind the Liberty bar on East Sixth Street has been serving these since it opened in 2010. They're symbolic of a scrappy and innovative time in Austin dining, when food trucks were just starting to take over.

They also happen to be very tasty. Lightly dusted with cornstarch, these beets are roasted and then deep-fried. Serve them with Kewpie mayo and a sprinkle of togarashi. And watch out: they're scaldingly hot straight out of the fryer.

Serves 6.

5 beets

2 tablespoons vegetable oil

2 tablespoons distilled white vinegar

Soybean oil for frying

1 cup (130 g) cornstarch

1 cup (120 ml) Kewpie mayonnaise (you can use regular mayo if you need to, but the Kewpie makes a big difference)

Shichimi togarashi (Japanese 7-spice blend)

2 scallions, thinly sliced

Salt

Heat the oven to 375°F (190°C).

Put the washed but unpeeled beets in a mixing bowl and toss them with the vegetable oil and vinegar. Place a large sheet of foil over a sheet pan and place the beets in the center of it. Place a second sheet of foil on top of the beets and crimp the edges of the two pieces of foil together to form an airtight packet. Roast for 1 hour 30 minutes to 2 hours, testing the beets for doneness by poking them with a small paring knife. Let the beets cool.

Peel the beets by rubbing off their skin with a paper towel or disposable gloves. Cut the beets into 1-inch (2.5-cm) cubes and chill thoroughly in the refrigerator, at least 1 hour.

Heat the soybean oil to 375°F (190°C) in a deep skillet.

Toss the beets in cornstarch until completely coated, and allow the beets to sit and absorb the cornstarch for a minute or so. The beets will be entirely magenta.

Fry the beets in 2-cup (270-g) batches until crispy, about 4 minutes per batch. Remove and drain on paper towels. Season with salt.

Serve with a squiggle of mayonnaise on top, along with a sprinkling of shichimi togarashi and scallion.

The Cadillac Bar Pie

Via 313

Via 313 started as a pizza truck, serving the Detroit-style pizza cofounders Zane and Brandon Hunt enjoyed while growing up in Michigan. Since then they have expanded both the pizza truck—now multiple trucks and brick-and-mortar restaurants—as well as the styles of pizza. This is a bar pie: a crispy, pan-baked round pie with a cheesy crust, topped with one of Via 313's most popular flavor combinations, the sweet-and-salty Cadillac.

For this one, you'll need a pizza stone and a round, 12-inch (30.5-cm) pizza pan (Hunt prefers the darkest pan you can find, nonstick anodized). Once you have those you'll be a pizza-making machine.

Makes 1 pizza.

- 1 ball prepared bar pie dough (recipe follows), plus flour for dusting
- ½ cup (120 ml) balsamic vinegar
- 1 ounce (28 g) asiago cheese, grated
- 6 ounces (170 g) whole-milk mozzarella, shredded
- ⅓ cup (45 g) crumbled gorgonzola cheese
- 2 tablespoons fig preserves
- 6 thin slices prosciutto
- Freshly grated Parmesan cheese

Two hours before you want to make the pizza, remove the dough from the fridge. One hour before you cook, put a pizza stone or baking steel in the middle rack of your oven and heat the oven to 500°F (260°C). Let the stone heat for the full hour.

Heat the vinegar in a small saucepan and bring it to a simmer. Cook until it is reduced by half, to a thick syrup. Let cool.

After the dough has rested for 2 hours at room temperature, sprinkle flour on a flat surface and use a rolling pin to roll out the ball into a 12-inch (30.5-cm) round. Move the dough to a lightly oiled 12-inch (30.5-cm) pizza pan. Sprinkle the asiago around the outside edge of the dough, and then cover the pizza with mozzarella and gorgonzola, spreading cheese to the edge of the pizza.

Put the pan on the pizza stone and bake for 12 minutes. The cheese should start to brown on the edges. Remove the pizza from the oven and transfer from the pizza pan to a cutting board.

Spread a thin layer of fig preserves over the pizza. Cut the pizza into 6 slices, and place a slice of prosciutto on top of each slice. Drizzle with about 1 tablespoon of the balsamic glaze and finish with a sprinkle of Parmesan.

Bar Pie Dough

Zane Hunt told me, "This is a lean-and-mean pizza dough, meant for home users to make delicious, no-frills pizza." It is, by far, the easiest pizza dough I have ever worked with. Hunt prefers weighing ingredients for the dough, but I've included cup measurements in case you don't have a scale.

Makes enough dough for 4 (12-inch/30.5-cm) pizzas.

6¼ cups (800 g) all-purpose flour
1 teaspoon (3 g) yeast
4 teaspoons (24 g) salt
1½ teaspoons (6 g) sugar
1⅓ cups (400 g) warm water
¼ cup (48 g) olive oil

Combine the flour and yeast in the bowl of a stand mixer.

In a separate bowl, dissolve the salt and sugar in the warm water. Add the oil.

With the mixer on low speed and the dough hook attached, slowly pour the liquid ingredients into the flour. Mix for 3 to 5 minutes, until the dough balls up on the hook.

Divide the dough into 4 pieces and shape the pieces into balls. Each ball should weigh about 200 grams, which will roll out perfectly in a 12-inch (30.5-cm) pan. Coat each ball lightly in oil and store covered in individual containers in the refrigerator overnight. (If you're using them the same day, leave them out at room temperature for at least 2 hours.) You can also freeze the dough at this point instead of refrigerating overnight. When ready to use, remove the dough from the freezer and let thaw, in the refrigerator, then rise at room temperature as instructed on the previous page.

Proceed as instructed for the Cadillac Bar Pie, or experiment with your own choice of toppings.

Oxtail Pappardelle with Rutabaga

Juniper

For years, Austinites bemoaned the lack of decent Italian food in town. Luckily there's been a wave of bright new pizza and pasta joints opening in recent years, among which Uchi alum Nicholas Yanes's Juniper is a standout.

This sophisticated, layered dish is more complicated than your standard, at-home ragu, but believe me, every step is worth it. In fact, you may as well double the ragu recipe—the leftovers will freeze very nicely.

Serves 6.

1 tablespoon vegetable oil

1 small rutabaga, peeled and diced

2 teaspoons chopped fresh rosemary

Salt

1 cup (240 ml) oxtail ragu (recipe follows)

½ cup (120 ml) ricotta

1 pound (455 g) good-quality pappardelle pasta

Black pepper

1 tablespoon chopped fresh herbs (parsley, basil, and/or chives)

Heat the vegetable oil in a sauté pan over medium-high heat, then sauté the rutabaga until lightly browned. Add rosemary and salt to taste; set aside.

Bring a pot of salted water to a boil. While the water heats up, put the ragu and ricotta in a sauté pan and stir to combine. Cook the pasta according to the package's instructions, then add it to the sauce.

Sauté the sauce and pasta over medium heat until the pasta is well coated, then add the rutabaga and combine. Season to taste with salt and pepper. Serve with chopped herbs on top.

Oxtail Ragu

Makes about 3 quarts (2.8 L).

3 pounds (1.4 kg) oxtail,
    cut into thick slices

Salt

2 cups (285 g) diced carrots

2 cups (220 g) diced onions

1¼ cups (300 ml) red wine

6 garlic cloves

1 sprig fresh rosemary

1 tablespoon juniper berries

2 bay leaves

2 teaspoons black peppercorns

2 cans (28 ounces/794 g each)
    whole San Marzano tomatoes

Black pepper

Season the pieces of oxtail liberally with salt and place them on a roasting pan. Refrigerate overnight.

Heat the oven to 450°F (230°C). Roast the oxtails until golden brown, 30 to 40 minutes. Add the carrots and onions to the pan around the oxtails and roast until the onions are browned, another 30 to 40 minutes. Be careful not to let the vegetables burn.

Put the browned meat and vegetables in a large pot. Use the wine to deglaze the roasting pan, scraping up any brown bits stuck to the pan. Add the wine to the pot.

Tie the garlic, rosemary, juniper berries, bay leaves, and peppercorns in a piece of cheesecloth and add this to the pot along with the tomatoes. Add water to cover by 1 inch (2.5 cm) or so. Cover and simmer for about 8 hours. Check the braise periodically to make sure the meat is still covered with liquid; if not, add water. When the meat is meltingly tender, let cool, remove the cheesecloth sachet, and remove the meat from the liquid.

Strain the braising liquid into another pot, making sure to press the vegetables to get as much liquid from them as you can. Bring to a simmer and cook until the liquid is reduced by about one-third, skimming the fat and impurities off the top as it reduces. Pick the oxtail meat from the bones, removing any gristle-y bits as you go. Add the picked meat to the reduced liquid and season with salt and ground pepper.

Duck Confit with Lemon Vinaigrette Frisée and Duck Fat–Roasted Potatoes

Justine's

Justine's is an energetic French bistro, a vintage house tucked away in the middle of an East Austin warehouse district. Not the most likely spot for a hip restaurant, but the place oozes with charm and draws diners from all over the city. It doesn't hurt that the wine list is fun and varied, the patio is large and pleasant, and the food is probably the best classic French in town.

Serve the following three elements together or separately for a taste of Paris by way of East Austin.

Serves 4.

2 tablespoons salt

2 tablespoons black pepper

4 duck legs

2 quarts (2 L) duck fat (if duck fat is not available, peanut, canola, or grapeseed oil will work)

Lemon vinaigrette frisée (recipe opposite)

Duck fat–roasted potatoes (recipe opposite)

Combine the salt and pepper in a small bowl. Place the duck legs in a shallow dish and thickly coat them with the salt and pepper mixture. Allow the meat to cure, uncovered, in the refrigerator for 24 hours.

Heat the oven to 300°F (150°C).

Brush most of the seasoning off the duck legs and place them in a deep, oven-safe cooking vessel that holds them snugly, like a medium Dutch oven. Cover the meat with duck fat—the legs must be completely submerged. Cook for 3 hours, then let the legs cool in the fat.

To serve, heat a cast-iron pan over medium heat. Add a bit of the duck fat and heat the duck legs skin side down until the skin is very crispy, about 8 minutes. Serve with the frisée and potatoes.

Lemon Vinaigrette Frisée

¼ cup (60 ml) Dijon mustard

¼ cup (60 ml) fresh lemon juice

1 teaspoon black pepper

1 teaspoon fresh thyme leaves

1 cup (240 ml) vegetable oil

Salt

3 cups (170 g) frisée

Put the mustard, lemon juice, pepper, and thyme in a food processor or blender and process until combined. With the processor running, slowly stream in the oil followed by ¼ cup (60 ml) water, processing until nice and creamy. Season with salt.

To serve, toss the frisée in a small amount of the dressing to lightly coat.

Duck Fat–Roasted Potatoes

6 red potatoes, quartered

¼ cup (60 ml) duck fat from the duck confit (recipe opposite)

Salt and black pepper

Heat the oven to 375°F (190°C).

Put the potatoes and duck fat in a large bowl and stir to coat the potatoes in fat. Season lightly with salt and pepper.

Roast on a sheet pan until tender for about 1 hour, shuffling and flipping the potatoes often so they brown evenly.

Chorizo Potato Pizza

Bufalina

This pizza, served at Steven Dilley's pizzeria Bufalina, is a bit more Texan than Neapolitan. Dilley told me, "This was inspired by one of my favorite breakfast tacos: chorizo, potato, and cheese. It's something I pick up from Veracruz All-Natural regularly." Breakfast taco pizza? Yes, please. (Check out the recipe for Veracruz's breakfast tacos on page 159.)

Makes 1 (12-inch/30.5-cm) pizza.

¼ cup (60 ml) red wine vinegar

1 teaspoon sugar

½ teaspoon salt

¼ cup (30 g) thinly sliced red onion

½ cup (100 g) chorizo

1 small russet potato, peeled and cut into ¼-inch (6-mm) dice (about ½ cup)

Salt

1 ball Neapolitan pizza dough (recipe follows), plus flour for dusting

3½ ounces (100 g) fresh mozzarella cheese, cut into short, thin strips

¼ cup (35 g) sliced pickled jalapeños (page 226 or store-bought)

1 tablespoon fresh oregano or parsley leaves

1 tablespoon crema

Place an oven rack in the top third of your oven, and put a pizza stone on it. Heat the oven as high as it will go (500 to 550°F/260 to 285°C) for 45 to 60 minutes. (If your oven has a convection roast cycle, use that.)

Whisk together the vinegar, ¼ cup (60 ml) water, the sugar, and salt, and pour the liquid over the onion. Refrigerate the onion mixture while you prepare the other ingredients.

Cook the chorizo in a skillet over medium-high heat, using a wooden spoon to break up the clumps of meat, until browned, about 4 minutes. Remove the meat with a slotted spoon and set aside, leaving the rendered fat in the pan.

Turn the heat to low and add the diced potato. Cook until the potato starts to soften, 8 to 10 minutes. Turn the heat back up to medium-high and cook until the potato is crisp and brown, 2 minutes. Season with salt. Set aside.

RECIPE CONTINUES ⟶

Assemble the pizza: Lightly flour a work surface. Gently stretch out the ball of pizza dough: first use your fingertips to press it out to about 6 inches (15 cm) in diameter, then use the backs of your hands to stretch it to 12 inches (30.5 cm) in diameter. Carefully place the dough on a lightly floured pizza peel; it will be pretty sticky.

Once it's on the peel, top it with the cheese, cooked chorizo, and crispy potatoes, spreading everything evenly over the dough.

Carefully slide the pizza from the peel onto the pizza stone. Bake for about 8 minutes. Remove the pizza from the oven and add the pickled red onion, the pickled jalapeño, and oregano. Dress with crema and let the pizza sit for a couple minutes before cutting it into slices.

Neapolitan Pizza Dough

This dough is more delicate than the bar pizza dough (page 129) and takes longer to rise. Plan ahead: if you start it at breakfast, you'll have pizza for dinner.

Makes enough dough for 2 (12-inch/30.5-cm) pizzas.

- 1 cup plus 1 tablespoon (250 g) warm water
- 2¼ teaspoons (13 g) salt
- 1 teaspoon (4 g) fresh cake yeast (or ¼ teaspoon dried yeast, but cake is preferred)
- 2¼ cups (450 g) 00 flour, such as Caputo or San Felice brand

In the bowl of a stand mixer, stir the warm water and salt together until the salt dissolves. Add the yeast and stir to dissolve. Add half of the flour and mix on the lowest speed for 2 minutes using the paddle attachment. Swap the paddle for the dough hook attachment and add the remaining flour. Mix on the lowest speed for 8 minutes. Remove the bowl from the mixer and let rise, covered with a damp cloth, for 2 hours. Note: at this stage it won't rise very much.

Divide the dough into two 250- to 260-gram portions. (You'll have a little dough left over, probably.) Form each portion into a ball. Place the balls in a container covered loosely with plastic wrap and allow to rise slowly at room temperature for 6 to 8 hours. Proceed with the instructions for the Potato Chorizo Pizza.

Sunshine Roll

Kome

Kome is located in a nondescript building on a busy stretch of Airport Boulevard. It would be easy to miss, if not for the throngs of people waiting outside for dinner every day. Their sushi is incredibly popular, not just in the neighborhood, but throughout the city. According to the restaurant, this is one of their most popular rolls, and it's as bright and lovely as the name implies.

Makes about 8 rolls.

For the sushi rice

2 cups (410 g) sushi rice

¼ cup (60 ml) rice vinegar

1 tablespoon sugar

1 teaspoon salt

In a mesh strainer, rinse the rice until the water runs clear. Put the rice in a saucepan with 2 cups (280 ml) water and bring to a boil. Once boiling, cover and reduce the heat to low. Cook for 15 minutes, then remove from the heat and let stand, covered, for another 10 minutes. (Alternatively, you could cook the rice in a rice cooker.)

Combine the vinegar, sugar, and salt. Put the warm cooked rice in a bowl—they use a dampened wooden bowl at Kome to prevent sticking—and pour the vinegar mixture over the top. Incorporate the seasoning into the rice with a spatula, cutting through and flipping sections of the rice until every grain is coated. Let cool for an additional 15 minutes, then flip the rice with a spatula a few more times. Let rest for another 10 minutes and the rice is ready to go.

For the rolls

4 sheets nori (seaweed paper)

2 tablespoons sesame seeds

½ mango, cut into strips ½ inch (12 mm) wide

½ avocado, cut into diagonal slices ¼ inch (6 mm) thick

6 ounces fresh, high-quality salmon, cut into strips ½ inch (12 mm) wide

Have the rice and all the ingredients ready. Place the nori on a sushi rolling mat and spread about ½ cup (105 g) of the rice over it, making sure every corner is covered. Sprinkle sesame seeds over the rice and flip everything over, so the nori side is facing up.

In a strip down the center of the nori, lay down a row of avocado first, then mango, and then salmon, making sure everything reaches all the way end to end. Use the sushi mat to roll and shape the sushi—the rice will be on the outside—then cut the roll into 6 pieces and serve.

Tom Kha Gai

Sway

In the heat of Texas summer, sometimes only food from another scaldingly hot part of the world will do. Yes, even soup. This flavorful version of the popular soup from the elegant modern Thai restaurant Sway will more than do the trick. Note: if you're in a hurry, you could use a rotisserie chicken from the grocery store instead of roasting it yourself.

Serves 8.

1 whole chicken

Salt and black pepper

¼ cup (60 ml) vegetable oil, plus more for frying shallots

1 head of garlic, cloves peeled and chopped

¼ cup (30 g) peeled and chopped galangal

4 stalks lemongrass, outer layers removed, chopped

6 to 8 Thai chiles, depending on how spicy you like it, thinly sliced

2½ quarts (2.5 L) chicken stock

1 cup (240 ml) fresh lime juice

2½ cups (600 g) palm sugar

1¼ cups (300 ml) fish sauce

2 cans (13½ ounces/398 ml each) coconut milk

1 cup (115 g) thinly sliced shallots

8 ounces (225 g) snow peas, trimmed

8 ounces (225 g) shimeji (beech) mushrooms, cut off the base so the stems separate

1 can (15 ounces/425 g) baby corn, drained

1 can (8 ounces/227 g) bamboo shoots, drained

¼ cup (60 ml) chile oil

Heat the oven to 325°F (165°C).

Season the chicken all over with salt and black pepper. Put in a roasting pan and roast for about 1 hour 30 minutes, or until its juices run clear. Let cool completely, then pull the meat into bite-size pieces and set aside. (Discard the bones and skin and gristle-y bits.)

While the chicken is roasting, heat the vegetable oil in a large pot over medium heat and add the garlic, galangal, lemongrass, and chiles. Sauté until the vegetables are soft, 8 to 10 minutes. Add the stock, lime juice, palm sugar, fish sauce, coconut milk, and 2 tablespoons salt, bring to a simmer, then reduce the heat and simmer for 10 minutes. Pour through a strainer into another large pot and set aside.

Heat about ½ inch (12 mm) of vegetable oil in a skillet over medium-low heat and add the shallots. Cook, stirring occasionally, until the shallots are lightly golden, about 12 minutes. Remove with a slotted spoon to a paper towel–lined plate. (The shallots will get darker after they're pulled from the oil, so pull them before they're as dark as you'd like.)

The previous steps can be done in advance. The stock will hold in the refrigerator for up to a week, and for several months frozen, while the shallots can be stored in an airtight container in the pantry for a couple weeks. The next few steps should only be completed right before serving.

Bring the soup broth to a simmer and add the snow peas, mushrooms, baby corn, bamboo shoots, and chile oil. Cook until the vegetables soften, 5 to 8 minutes. Add the pulled chicken and season the soup with salt to taste. Serve with crispy shallots on top.

Grilled Quail with Green Mole

Lenoir

Texas is prime quail country, and these tiny birds are hunted throughout the state. Quail is good fried, but, as Todd Duplechan of Lenoir says, "Cooking little birds over wood or charcoal is just the best." I'm not going to argue with that. Typically quail come either bone-in or "semi-deboned," meaning all of the bones except the wings and legs have been removed for easier eating.

Serves 4.

8 semi-deboned quails
¼ cup (60 ml) vegetable oil
Salt and black pepper

For the sauce

4 garlic cloves, peeled and left whole
3 green tomatoes, cut in half
3 serrano chiles, stems removed
1 onion, cut in half and peeled
Salt
¾ cup (22 g) fresh basil leaves
¾ cup (22 g) fresh cilantro
¾ cup (22 g) fresh garlic chives
½ cup (65 g) pepitas (hulled pumpkin seeds)
½ cup (75 g) sesame seeds
1½ teaspoons black peppercorns
1 tablespoon coriander seeds
1½ teaspoons cumin seeds
1 teaspoon fenugreek seeds
¾ cup (180 ml) canola oil

RECIPE CONTINUES ⟶

Rub the quails with the oil and season them lightly with salt and pepper. Set them aside to come to room temperature while you make the sauce.

Make the sauce: Heat the broiler to high.

Put the garlic, tomatoes, serranos, and onion on a sheet pan and broil until roasted and nearly burned, checking periodically.

Bring a pot of salted water to a boil, and prepare a bowl of ice water next to it. When the water is boiling vigorously, add the basil, cilantro, and chives and blanch briefly—less than 10 seconds—until they turn a vibrant green, then use tongs or a slotted spoon to remove them from the boiling water. Immediately plunge them in the ice bath. This process locks in their color and gives the mole its vibrancy. Drain the herbs well.

Toast the pepitas and sesame seeds in a dry skillet and set aside. Separately, toast the peppercorns, coriander, cumin, and fenugreek; let cool, then grind them in a spice grinder.

Add the roasted vegetables, blanched herbs, seeds, and spices to a blender or food processor along with ½ cup (120 ml) water. Process to a thick paste (you can add a bit more water if things aren't moving), then slowly drizzle in the oil while the motor is on. You'll end up with a lush, thick, bright green sauce. Season with salt.

Heat a grill to high. Grill the quails until just cooked through, about 5 minutes per side. Serve two quails per person, with the sauce on the side.

Sauerkraut Johnnycakes

Emmer & Rye

This dish brings together two key components of chef Kevin Fink's Emmer & Rye: a focus on heritage grains, and the restaurant's in-house fermentation program. It's fairly simple to make, although it does benefit greatly from high-quality corn flour, sauerkraut, pancetta, and cheddar. Use this as a base for sautéed vegetables for a simple, elegant dinner.

Makes about 16 (4-inch/10-cm) pancakes.

1¼ cups (300 ml) whole milk

⅓ cup (75 ml) hot water

1 packet (3/4 ounce/21 g) active dry yeast

1½ cups (190 g) all-purpose flour

¾ cup (135 g) corn flour

1½ teaspoons salt

4 tablespoons (115 g) unsalted butter, melted

⅓ cup (80 g) finely diced pancetta

½ cup (75 g) sauerkraut

¾ cup (85 g) finely diced white cheddar cheese

3 tablespoons vegetable oil

Crème fraîche

Combine the milk and hot water; the liquid should be warm but not hot. Add the yeast and let stand for 15 minutes.

In a large bowl, combine the all-purpose flour, corn flour, and salt.

Fold the yeast mixture and the melted butter into the flour mixture with a spatula, taking care not to overwork the batter. Let rise for 30 minutes.

While the batter is rising, put the pancetta in a skillet and add ½ cup (120 ml) water. Cook over medium heat, stirring occasionally, until the water is gone and the pork just starts to sear, about 10 minutes—the idea is to cook the pancetta without crisping it up too much. Add the sauerkraut and a little bit of its brine to the skillet with the pancetta and stir, scraping up any bits of pancetta stuck to the pan. Remove from the heat and let cool completely.

Fold the pancetta and sauerkraut mixture and the cheese into the batter.

Heat the oil in a skillet. Drop 2 to 3 tablespoons of the batter into the hot pan for each pancake and cook, flipping as each side browns, 1 to 2 minutes per side. The center should be cooked through, not doughy, and the pancakes should be about 4 inches (10 cm) across. Serve with a dollop of crème fraîche.

Bakra Goat Burger

Whip-In

The Whip-In's evolution from gas station to South Austin landmark began in 1986 when it was purchased by the Topiwala family. Since then, the space has morphed into a bar and restaurant known for a great beer selection and their signature blend of Indian and Texan food, like migas with cilantro chutney and this burger, made with spiced ground goat meat and a homemade chile aioli.

Makes 8 burgers.

For the burgers

3 pounds (1.4 kg) ground goat meat

⅔ cup (150 g) minced yellow onion

1½ tablespoons minced garlic

1½ tablespoons minced ginger

½ cup (20 g) finely chopped fresh cilantro

6 jalapeños, roasted (see page 94), seeds and stems removed, and finely chopped

2 teaspoons kosher salt

1 teaspoon black pepper

For serving

Squishy white hamburger buns, toasted

Goat milk feta cheese

Mixed greens

Sliced cherry tomatoes

Indian long chile aioli (recipe follows)

RECIPE CONTINUES ⟶

Make the burgers: Combine the goat meat, onion, garlic, ginger, cilantro, jalapeños, salt, and black pepper in a large mixing bowl using very clean hands. Shape the mixture into 8 equal-size burger patties. Cook the patties in a hot cast-iron skillet or on a grill until cooked through but not dry, 5 to 6 minutes on each side. Let the burgers rest for about 5 minutes before serving.

Serve on toasted buns topped with cheese, greens, tomatoes, and aioli.

Indian Long Chile Aioli

1 egg yolk

1 garlic clove, coarsely chopped

1 teaspoon salt

2 teaspoons fresh lemon juice

⅓ cup (75 ml) canola oil

⅓ cup (75 ml) olive oil

2 Indian long chiles, seeds and stem removed, finely diced (Thai chiles will work if you can't find long chiles)

Put the egg yolk, garlic, salt, and lemon juice in a food processor or blender and process for about 30 seconds, until thoroughly mixed. With the processor on, slowly drizzle the oils into the yolk mixture. When finished, fold in the chiles and serve. Store, covered, in the refrigerator for up to a week.

Pig Skin Noodles with Shrimp Dumplings and Hot Sauce

Barley Swine

This dish has been on the menu at Bryce Gilmore's flagship restaurant ever since they moved it from the original space to its current dreamy location on Burnet Road. The restaurant preserves chiles all summer so they can keep this dish on the menu year round. "I like having a few interesting items that stick around for a long time," says Gilmore, "for people to enjoy and rely on."

Don't be afraid of the pig skin: this is one of Barley Swine's most popular dishes for a reason. Long, noodle-like strands of pig skin are simmered until tender, then tossed with a house-made hot sauce, shrimp dumplings, and almonds for a combination that's reminiscent of a rice noodle bowl.

Serves 6.

½ cup (120 g) plus 1 teaspoon salt

2 cups (480 ml) hot water

2 pounds (910 g) pork skin

1 pound (450 g) peeled and deveined shrimp, tails removed

2 eggs

1 garlic clove, grated or pressed

1 Thai chile, seeded and coarsely chopped

½ cup (120 ml) Hot Sauce (page 227)

½ cup (55 g) slivered almonds, toasted

RECIPE CONTINUES ⟶

Brine the pork skin: Dissolve ½ cup (120 g) salt in the hot water and allow the mixture to cool to room temperature. Put the pork skin in a gallon-size (3.8-L-size) resealable bag and add the brine; refrigerate for at least 4 hours or overnight.

Drain the pork skin and pat it lightly with paper towels to dry. Roll it into a tight cylinder; wrap the cylinder tightly with plastic wrap and put it in the freezer until firm but not frozen, about 1 hour.

While you're waiting on the pork skin, make the dumplings: Put the shrimp, eggs, garlic, chile, and 1 teaspoon salt in a food processor and process until smooth. Form the shrimp mixture into small, round dumplings, about 1 tablespoon each.

Bring two pots of water to a simmer. Remove the pork skin from the freezer and slice it into thin, long noodles. Simmer the noodles in one of the pots until tender, about 30 minutes. (The noodles should be about the consistency of a rice noodle when finished.) Set about ½ cup (120 ml) of the cooking liquid aside, then drain the pork skin noodles.

In the other pot, when the noodles are almost finished, simmer the shrimp dumplings until just cooked through, about 5 minutes. Drain.

To finish the dish, combine the noodles and the dumplings in a sauté pan. Add the hot sauce and a bit of the noodle cooking liquid to make a sauce and heat, stirring, for about 2 minutes to combine. Serve in bowls, sprinkled with the almonds.

Sweet Potato Nachos

Odd Duck

Odd Duck is Bryce Gilmore's second restaurant, although it evolved from a prior effort: the Odd Duck Farm to Trailer food truck. In one of my favorite bits of Austin restaurant trivia, the current Odd Duck brick-and-mortar restaurant is built on the land where the trailer once stood. How's that for coming full circle?

This dish gets its name from the nacho spice blend that flavors the sweet potatoes, which are then dotted with green chile mayo, escabeche, and corn nuts. It's a bit of work, but this would make a killer dinner party dish served alongside a simple roast chicken.

Serves 6 to 8 as a side.

4 large sweet potatoes

½ cup (120 ml) vegetable oil

Salt

2 teaspoons nacho spice (recipe follows)

2 tablespoons unsalted butter

¼ cup (60 ml) green chile mayo (recipe follows)

½ cup (75 g) escabeche (recipe follows)

½ cup (80 g) corn nuts (recipe follows; optional)

¼ cup (30 g) thinly sliced radish

¼ cup (10 g) chopped fresh cilantro

Heat the oven to 325°F (165°C).

Bake the sweet potatoes whole on a foil-lined sheet pan until tender, about 1 hour. Let cool completely.

Peel the sweet potatoes (you can probably do it with your fingers) and set the peels aside. Cut the potatoes into large chunks, about 2-inch (5-cm) pieces.

Heat the oil in a small sauté pan. Fry the peels until crispy, taking care not to burn them. Remove from the oil and set on paper towels to drain. When cool, sprinkle the peels with a pinch of salt and 1 teaspoon nacho spice. (Up through this step, everything can be made the day before.)

Heat a large sauté pan over medium heat; add the butter and cook until it has browned slightly. Add the sweet potatoes and cook to heat through, about 3 minutes, then season with salt.

Place the hot sweet potatoes in a serving dish that holds them snugly and smash them partially with a fork. In the following order, dot the potatoes with the green chile mayo, then sprinkle with escabeche, corn nuts (if using), fried peels, radish, cilantro, and a light sprinkle of nacho spice. Serve immediately.

Nacho Spice

Makes about ½ cup (48 g).

2 tablespoons ground cumin

2 tablespoons ground coriander

1 tablespoon nutritional yeast

2 teaspoons ground bay leaves

Combine all the ingredients and store in an airtight container.

Green Chile Mayo

1 cup (240 ml) grapeseed oil

1 poblano, seeded and diced

1 teaspoon red chile flakes

1 egg yolk

1 teaspoon Dijon mustard

1 tablespoon distilled white vinegar

Salt

Heat the oil in a small sauté pan over medium-low heat. Add the poblano and cook for 10 minutes, keeping an eye on it to make sure nothing burns. Remove from the heat and add the chile flakes. Let cool completely, then pour the oil through a strainer set over a bowl; discard the solids.

In a food processor or blender, combine the egg yolk, mustard, and vinegar. Slowly—drop by drop at first, and then in increasing amounts—add the chile oil. You should have a thick, pale green sauce when you're done. Season with salt. Store, covered, in the refrigerator for up to five days.

Escabeche

½ bay leaf

1 teaspoon coriander seeds

½ teaspoon cumin seeds

1 whole dried chipotle pepper

½ cup (120 ml) apple cider vinegar

¼ cup (60 ml) distilled white vinegar

2 tablespoons brown sugar

2 tablespoons grapeseed oil

1½ tablespoons salt

1 onion, sliced

1 carrot, sliced

2 sprigs fresh oregano

In a dry skillet, toast the bay leaf, coriander, cumin, and chipotle until fragrant. Tie the spices in a piece of cheesecloth.

In a sauté pan over medium heat, bring the vinegars, 2 tablespoons water, the brown sugar, and the spice packet to a boil. Add the oil, salt, onion, and carrot and stir until the salt dissolves, about 1 minute. Remove from the heat, add the oregano, and let cool completely. Remove the spice packet after cooling. Refrigerate until chilled before serving.

Corn Nuts

The corn here is important: it is not popcorn, it is not dehydrated corn, it is not freeze-dried corn, it's dried corn. It is easier to find in the fall at seasonal markets and the like, but you can order it online year round. Pickling lime can be found wherever you buy canning supplies, or ordered online as well.

Since these are a bit of work, it's worth it to make a bunch. They'll keep in an airtight container in the pantry for a couple weeks and make for great snacking if you're not using them to garnish the Sweet Potato Nachos.

    1 cup (200 g) dried corn

    1 tablespoon pickling lime

    Vegetable oil for frying

    Salt

    1 teaspoon nacho spice (recipe opposite)

Put the dried corn and lime in a nonreactive pot. Add water to cover by about 2 inches (5 cm).

Bring to a simmer and cook for 45 minutes. At this point, remove a kernel and cut it in half crosswise to check if it's done—you want it to be about three-quarters gel and one-quarter starch in the very center. If it's not there yet, cook it for another 10 minutes and check again. When the kernels are three-quarters gel, remove from the heat and let the corn sit at room temperature in the lime solution for at least 12 hours. Note: Lime water is caustic and should be kept out of reach of kids and pets. Make sure to leave it covered and out of reach.

The next day, drain and rinse the corn at least three times in a strainer—you need to remove every last trace of lime. Put the corn in a mixer with the paddle attachment and mix slowly for about 5 minutes. (This helps the husks to loosen.) Return to the strainer and rub off the husks while running under water.

When you're ready to make the corn nuts, rinse the prepared kernels. Boil them for 30 minutes, or until slightly overcooked. Rinse and dry very well (in a salad spinner or on paper towels).

Heat oil in a medium pot to 375°F (190°C). Fry the kernels until the bubbles subside, about 5 minutes, then remove to drain on paper towels. Season with salt and nacho spice.

CHAPTER

BREAKFAST

AND

BRUNCH

In Search of a Perfect Breakfast Taco

Austin's breakfast tacos are the stuff of legend. We aren't the only Texas city that claims them—hi, San Antonio—and Texans were certainly not the first people to serve eggs wrapped in a tortilla. But Austin takes breakfast tacos to the next level. They are both the building blocks of this city and one of its highest art forms.

It's a deceptively SIMPLE concept: combine a few breakfast ingredients (eggs, bacon, cheese) in a tortilla, apply salsa, cure hangover, move on with your day. But if they're so simple, why are they so tricky to master?

It's because of that simplicity that every element must be entirely on point. The tortillas must be fresh and hot, the salsa scalding and flavorful, and the ingredients masterfully paired. Thought must be given to whether certain ingredients are best cooked into the egg (chorizo, jalapeños), or better sprinkled on top (cheese, avocado). If any of these elements miss the mark, the taco will fall flat—and believe me, there are few things worse than a bad breakfast taco.

Thankfully there is an expert on what makes for the PERFECT breakfast taco: YOU. The best breakfast tacos are the ones you order to your particular, discerning tastes. Often, breakfast counters and taco trucks will simply have a long list of ingredients, with prices given for two-ingredient tacos and three-ingredient tacos. It is up to you to become the architect of the breakfast tacos of your dreams.

To illustrate, here's a list of breakfast taco ingredients, compiled from the restaurants and taco trucks in this book (plus a few extras). Experiment with them to see what you like. Once you've found a few combinations that speak to your early morning soul, it's time to go to breakfast taco graduate school. Branch out into egg-free breakfast tacos—no, breakfast tacos do not require eggs—or get crazy with your own unique ingredients and combinations. Just make sure, in all cases, that you use the freshest tortillas you can get your hands on.

(Or you can just skip all that and follow the instructions for expertly designed breakfast tacos from Veracruz All-Natural on the next page, or the migas from Mi Madres on page 168—your call.)

EGGS
(generally scrambled)

AMERICAN CHEESE

MONTEREY JACK CHEESE

Cheddar cheese

QUESO FRESCO

QUESO
(page 72)

BACON
(whole slices or chopped)

CHORIZO

SAUSAGE
(crumbled or chopped links)

STEAK

CHICKEN

HAM

MACHACADO
(shredded dried beef)

FRIED POTATOES
(cubed or shredded)

RICE

BLACK BEANS

PINTO BEANS
(page 42)

Refried beans
(page 76)

AVOCADO

GUACAMOLE
(page 75)

SPINACH

MUSHROOMS

RAJAS
(strips of poblano and onions,
grilled or sautéed)

SERRANO CHILE

ONION

TOMATO

JALAPEÑO

ONION, TOMATO, AND JALAPEÑO
(sometimes called "a la
Mexicana" or "a la mex")

CILANTRO

NOPALITOS
(strips of cactus paddle)

Potato and Sausage Breakfast Tacos

Veracruz All-Natural

Veracruz All-Natural is one of the best-loved taco trucks in Austin. They're so popular, in fact, they now have multiple trucks as well as brick-and-mortar restaurants. Sisters Reyna and Maritza Vazquez originally founded a smoothie stand that started selling food by customer request. The rest is taco history.

Veracruz is well known for its migas tacos (more on page 168), as well as its amazing breakfast tacos, like these. In fact, their breakfast tacos are responsible for inspiring Bufalina's Chorizo Potato Pizza (page 134). Now that is some taco.

Serves 2.

Salt

1½ cups (210 g) diced peeled potato (about 1 russet potato)

4 eggs

Black pepper

1 tablespoon vegetable oil

1 cup (about 1 link/125 g) sausage of your choice, cooked and diced

Corn or flour tortillas

½ cup (55 g) shredded Monterey Jack cheese

½ cup (55 g) diced onion

½ cup (20 g) chopped fresh cilantro

½ avocado, sliced

Salsa (like Veracruz's Salsa Macha Verde, page 223) or hot sauce

Bring a medium pot of salted water to a boil, add the potato, and cook until soft. Drain and let the potato cool.

Whisk the eggs thoroughly in a mixing bowl and season with a big pinch of salt and pepper.

Heat the oil in a pan over medium heat. Add the potato and cook until golden brown, about 3 minutes. Add the sausage and cook for another 2 minutes, until the sausage is browned. Add the eggs and scramble until cooked through but still slightly wet, then remove from the heat.

Heat the tortillas (see page 48), then add the egg mixture. Top the eggs with the cheese, onion, cilantro, and a slice of avocado each. Apply salsa or hot sauce to taste.

24 Hash

24 Diner

24 Diner is one of the few places in Austin where you can get a good solid breakfast any time of day. Important for students, touring musicians, and the occasional cookbook author. This is one of their classic dishes—a crispy, cheesy, meaty hash with eggs baked on top. This is great with leftover taco filling or barbecue instead of bacon and sausage, and it loves a hefty dash of hot sauce on top.

Serves 2 people, or 1 really hungry person.

4 ounces (115 g) bacon, cut into ¼-inch (6-mm) pieces

4 ounces (115 g) breakfast sausage

2 cups (280 g) diced unpeeled potatoes

Salt and black pepper

Olive oil as needed

½ onion, chopped

1 jalapeño, seeded and chopped

4 ounces (115 g) cheddar cheese, shredded

4 eggs

1 scallion, sliced

Heat the oven to 450°F (230°C).

In a 12-inch (30.5-cm) cast-iron skillet (or some other 12-inch/30.5-cm ovenproof pan), cook the bacon and sausage over medium heat until browned and crispy, stirring to break up the sausage. Use a slotted spoon to remove the meat from the pan and set it on a paper towel to drain the grease. Leave the leftover fat in the pan.

Toss the potatoes in the remaining fat, seasoning them with a bit of salt and black pepper. Transfer the skillet to the oven and bake the potatoes for 12 minutes, or until soft but not browned. Remove the potatoes from the pan with a slotted spoon and set aside.

You should have a tablespoon or two of bacon grease left in the pan; if not, add a bit of oil. Sauté the onion and jalapeño over medium heat until softened. In a mixing bowl, mix together the cooked bacon and sausage, potatoes, onion and jalapeño, and cheese.

Return the mixture to the pan and spread into an even layer. Use the back of a spoon to create four shallow wells in the potato mixture. Crack eggs into these wells and bake until the whites are set but the yolks are still runny, about 10 minutes. Remove from the oven and divide into individual servings using a metal spatula. Sprinkle with the scallion and serve.

Good Morning from East Austin

Regina Estrada is a third-generation restaurateur: her family's East Austin breakfast and lunch spot, Joe's Bakery, has been open since 1962. Here, in her own words, she explains how her rapidly gentrifying East Austin neighborhood may be changing, but the huevos rancheros stay the same.

We serve breakfast all day. That's what we do. We open at 6 a.m. and close at 2:30 p.m., and our breakfast menu, our tacos, we serve from 6 to 2:30.

We've always done handmade flour tortillas. It's one of the things we're known for. We make the bread here. We hand-cut the carne guisada. We sell our menudo every day. We used to serve biscuits, but that's because my grandfather used to make the biscuits.

Tejano music plays on our jukebox. I have some people come in, they will put on $5 worth of music—that's about twenty songs—and they will sit there the whole time and just listen to the music. They say, "I remember when I used to come here with my dad." It takes them back to an Austin that's disappearing. We're serving generations of a family at a table. You know what I mean?

Joe's Bakery officially went into business in 1962. The restaurant was opened by my grandfather, Joe Avila. But my great-grandparents sold bread out of their home since the '30s, and that's where my grandfather really got his interest in baking. We actually still have customers come in and say they remember buying the bread in the neighborhood when they were kids. Essentially, we've been in East Austin since about about 1930. We're very heavily rooted in the community.

My grandparents were both raised in Austin, and my grandfather was very proud of the fact that he was an American. He served in the military, he was in the Korean War. He had a Purple Heart. He was proud of his country.

He also held deep roots to his culture, to his heritage. He always wore a guayabera, which is the traditional Mexican shirt. That was his uniform, from when I was a little girl until he passed in 2011. That was part of him embracing his culture, saying, "Hey, this is me." I feel that's his greatest legacy: he was proud of where he came from and who he was. He embraced all of it.

After my grandfather got out of the army, he settled down with my grandmother, got married. When they started out, it was a small-time operation, just a bakery. We're talking a couple tables. You've got to think about back in the '60s. It was tough for anybody of color to get things rolling. In the history of Austin, everybody of color was east of Interstate

Huevos Rancheros

Joe's Bakery

Huevos rancheros: eggs how you want 'em, topped with ranchero sauce, served with tortillas on the side. Joe's adds beans to the plate, as well as a couple pieces of their famous crispy, lightly floured bacon, so I recommend you do the same. This recipe calls for sunny-side-up eggs, but if you prefer scrambled, go for it.

Serves 1.

1 tablespoon vegetable oil

2 eggs

Salt and black pepper

½ cup (120 ml) Ranchero Sauce (page 231)

Refried beans (page 76)

Bacon (page 165)

2 flour tortillas, warmed (see page 48)

Heat the oil in a skillet or nonstick pan over medium heat, and crack two eggs into it. Lower the heat slightly and cook the eggs until the whites are set but the yolks are still runny, 3 to 5 minutes. Season with salt and pepper.

While the eggs are cooking, heat the ranchero sauce in a small pan.

To serve, put the eggs on a plate and top with the ranchero sauce. Add the beans and bacon to the plate, and serve with flour tortillas on the side.

Migas

Mi Madres

"*Migas* is short for *migajas*," says Christina Milian-Torres of Mi Madres, "which means 'crumbs.'" Migas are often a way for restaurants to use up leftover chips and tortillas, but they're worth making for their own sake. After all, she says, they give "a great crunch to scrambled eggs."

You'll see migas on menus as a plate, served with beans and tortillas on the side, or served as tacos. Often you'll have an option to add cooked, crumbled chorizo as well, so if you're feeling it, go ahead and add some.

Serves 6.

10 eggs

Salt and black pepper

2 tablespoons vegetable oil

1 cup (40 g) corn tortillas cut into strips (stale tortillas are better)

½ cup (90 g) diced tomato

½ cup (55 g) diced onion

¼ cup (40 g) diced jalapeño

1 cup (115 g) shredded Monterey Jack and cheddar cheese blend

Whisk the eggs thoroughly in a mixing bowl, season with a pinch of salt and black pepper, and set aside.

Heat the oil in a pan over medium heat. Add the tortilla strips and sauté briefly, until they get a bit crunchy, 1 to 2 minutes. Add the tomato, onion, and jalapeño and sauté until the onion has softened somewhat, 2 to 3 minutes.

Add the eggs and use a spatula to turn the mixture while it's cooking, making sure the tortilla strips stay whole. Once the eggs are cooked, remove from the heat and sprinkle with the cheese. Serve when the cheese has just melted.

Texas Benedict

Frank

If it weren't abundantly clear already, Texans have a habit of Texifying things. Here, Frank restaurant Texifies that old brunch standby, eggs Benedict. What that means: cheddar biscuits replace the English muffins, braised pork stands in for Canadian bacon, the eggs are fried instead of poached, and the whole thing is smothered in a spicy jalapeño hollandaise.

Serves 8.

1 tablespoon vegetable oil

8 eggs

Salt and black pepper

4 Cheddar Biscuits (page 198), warm

2 cups (200 g) Basic Braised Pork for Tacos (page 51), warm (see Note)

Jalapeño hollandaise (recipe follows)

1 small bunch scallions, sliced

Paprika

Heat the oil in a skillet over medium heat. Fry the eggs, working in batches if necessary, until the whites are set but the yolks are still runny. Season with salt and pepper.

To assemble the benedicts: Cut a warm biscuit in half. Top each half with ¼ cup (65 g) pulled pork, 1 fried egg, and a large spoonful of hollandaise. Sprinkle with scallions and a bit of paprika and serve.

__Note__: Prepare the Basic Braised Pork for Tacos, substituting 2 good longneck beers of choice for some of the water. You may also add 1 tablespoon ground chile and 1 tablespoon granulated garlic powder to the seasoning.

Jalapeño Hollandaise

1 cup (240 ml) clarified butter
(see Note), warm

1 egg yolk

2 jalapenos, roasted (page 94)
with seeds, skin, and stem
removed

Squeeze of lemon juice

Pinch of cayenne pepper

Salt

Warm the clarified butter over low heat in a saucepan, but do not bring it all the way to a simmer.

Place the jalapenos and the egg yolks in a blender and blend briefly.

Very, very slowly, with the blender running on a medium speed, drizzle the clarified butter into the egg yolk mixture. Add the lemon juice and cayenne and blend briefly to combine. You should end up with a thick, light sauce—thick enough to coat a spoon, but not runny. If it's too thick, add a teaspoon or two of warm water and blend to combine. Season the sauce with salt. Serve immediately.

Note: Clarified butter is butter that has had the milk solids removed. You can buy clarified butter in the store, but it's easy enough to make at home. Heat the butter in a saucepan over low heat until melted. You'll notice some solids forming at both the top and the bottom of the liquid; you want to discard these and keep only the golden liquid in between. Skim off the top solids with a spoon, then slowly pour the golden liquid through a strainer into a heatproof container, making sure to leave the milky white substance behind in the saucepan.

Pumpkin Bread French Toast

Kerbey Lane

Kerbey Lane has been slinging breakfast, lunch, dinner, and queso since 1980. It was one of the first restaurants in Austin to start changing the menu seasonally, which makes this recipe an autumnal treat. The pumpkin bread for the French toast is made from scratch, and while it's super easy to make, you might want to plan ahead on this one.

Serves 4 to 6.

4 eggs
¾ cup (180 ml) buttermilk
¾ cup (180 ml) 2% milk
½ teaspoon ground cinnamon
2 teaspoons sugar
½ tablespoon vanilla extract
1 loaf Pumpkin Bread (page 197)
4 tablespoons (55 g) unsalted butter
Powdered sugar

In a mixing bowl, whisk the eggs thoroughly. Whisk in the buttermilk and milk, then whisk in the cinnamon, sugar, and vanilla.

Heat a griddle or skillet over medium heat and add a small amount of the butter.

Cut the pumpkin bread into slices 1 inch (2.5 cm) thick. Dip the slices into the egg mixture and keep the bread submerged for 2 or 3 seconds, so the batter soaks into the bread. Cook the slices of bread in the skillet until golden brown, 2 to 3 minutes per side.

Cut each slice of French toast in half diagonally and serve dusted with powdered sugar.

Gingerbread Pancakes

Magnolia Cafe

The sign out front reads, "Sorry, We're Open," and they mean it. Open all the time, every day, Magnolia Cafe is where you go for bowls of Mag Mud (a white queso with black beans, avocado, and pico de gallo), endless coffee, and pancakes the size of your head.

While Magnolia serves several types of pancakes, this gingerbread version, spiked with coffee and spices and laced with buttermilk, is a crowd favorite. You can make them Magnolia-style—that is, giant—or normal pancake sized.

Serves 6.

4 eggs

¼ cup (55 g) brown sugar

½ cup (120 ml) buttermilk

¼ cup (60 ml) brewed coffee

2½ cups (320 g) all-purpose flour

2½ teaspoons baking powder

2 teaspoons baking soda

1 teaspoon ground cloves

1 tablespoon ground cinnamon

1 tablespoon ginger powder

1 tablespoon grated nutmeg

6 tablespoons (85 g) unsalted butter, melted, plus more for cooking the pancakes

Maple syrup, for serving

Whisk the eggs together in a mixing bowl, then whisk in the brown sugar. Add the buttermilk, ½ cup plus 3 tablespoons (160 ml) water, and the coffee. Whisk to combine.

In another mixing bowl, sift together the flour, baking powder, baking soda, cloves, cinnamon, ginger, and nutmeg. Add the dry ingredients to the wet ingredients and stir until just combined, then add the melted butter. Stir briefly to bring everything together.

Heat a frying pan or a griddle over medium heat, then add a small amount of butter. Pour about ⅓ cup (75 ml) batter per pancake into the pan and cook until each side is golden, 1 to 2 minutes per side. (Flip the pancakes when you start to see bubbles forming on the surface.) You can keep the cooked pancakes warm in a 250°F (120°C) oven while you cook the remaining batches.

<u>Note</u>: This recipe makes normal-size pancakes, but if you want giant, Magnolia-size pancakes, simply double how much batter you pour in the pan for each pancake. And be careful when flipping them.

Beef Tongue Empanadas
Salt and Time

What started as a farmers' market charcuterie stand in 2010 has blown up into a busy restaurant and one of Austin's premier meat markets. This recipe is from Salt and Time's brunch menu, although you could really make this any time of day. If you're afraid of beef tongue (do not be afraid of beef tongue; it is delicious and beefy), you could sub in basic pulled pork (page 51) or leftover barbecue (chapter 1).

Makes about 12 empanadas.

For the filling

2 quarts (2 L) lightly salted stock or water

1 beef tongue (2 to 3 pounds/910 g to 1.4 kg)

2 to 3 tablespoons lard or butter

1 small white onion, diced

3 to 4 garlic cloves, chopped

2 tablespoons flour

Salt and black pepper

For the dough

4 cups (450 g) masa flour

1 teaspoon ground cumin

1 teaspoon granulated garlic powder

1 teaspoon onion powder

1 teaspoon salt

3 cups (720 ml) warm stock or water

Vegetable oil for deep-frying

Crème fraîche, thinly sliced radishes, chopped fresh cilantro, and hot sauce

Make the filling: Bring the stock to a boil in a medium pot with a lid. Reduce the heat to a simmer, add the beef tongue, and cover. Simmer until tender, 3 hours.

Let the tongue cool in the braising liquid. When cool enough to handle, remove the tongue from the pot, reserving the liquid for later. Remove the outer membrane of the tongue with a sharp knife—if you're lucky, it will peel off easily—then dice the meat into ¼-inch (6-mm) pieces.

Heat the lard in a large skillet over medium heat. Add the onion and sauté until translucent, 3 to 5 minutes. Add the garlic and sauté for 3 to 4 minutes, until everything is fragrant and soft.

Lower the heat to medium-low. Add the flour and stir to combine, then add 1¼ cups (300 ml) of the braising liquid. Add the tongue and simmer until the mixture begins to thicken, 2 minutes. Season with salt and pepper, then remove from the heat. Let cool.

Make the dough: Combine the masa, cumin, garlic powder, onion powder, and salt in a large mixing bowl. Add the stock slowly and knead until a nice, smooth dough forms. This dough dries out quickly; keep it covered with a moist paper towel or cloth when you're not working with it. You want it to be the consistency of clay.

Portion the dough into 2-inch (5-cm) balls. Using a rolling pin, flatten the balls between two sheets of waxed paper, until you have circles that are ⅛ inch (3 mm) thick.

Put 2 tablespoons of the filling in the center of each circle. Fold the circle in half to form a half-moon, and press the edges together to seal. At this point the empanadas can be stored for up to 2 days in a sealed container, refrigerated, covered with a moist paper towel or cloth.

When you're ready to fry the empanadas, fill a large, heavy-bottomed skillet with oil 1 to 2 inches (2.5 to 5 cm) deep. Heat the oil to 325°F (165°C) and fry the empanadas until golden brown, about 3 minutes per side. Serve with crème fraîche, radishes, cilantro, and hot sauce.

CHAPTER 7

DRINKS

This is the scene, year round, no matter the weather: The backyard of a bar, or maybe a deck out front facing the street, lined with picnic tables. Maybe there's a band, maybe there's a jukebox. Maybe there's a food truck with a line snaking through the crowd. There are definitely tons of people talking, laughing, yelling, singing, arguing. The tables are crowded with beer bottles, and servers weave their way through the crowd carrying towers of empty pint glasses. Friends offer to buy each other rounds: pint of Lone Star, pint of Pearl Snap, two Live Oak hefes, a whiskey diet, and one of those spicy margarita things, right?

For better or for worse, Austin is a bar town. But hey, you don't get to be the Live Music Capital of the World without slinging a few shots. Thankfully, the Austin cocktail scene has grown up a bit since Guy Clark sang about drinking those cheaper-than-dirt Mad Dog Margaritas at the Texas Chili Parlor.

While you can still get a good deal on pitchers of Lone Star around town, they're served alongside pitchers of craft beer. Many bars now cater to a more discerning clientele, serving craft cocktails, Texas wines, and beers from Austin's robust local brewing scene. That doesn't mean every bar has gone highbrow—you can still get those giant, electric-colored flavored margaritas served in pint glasses. But now, sometimes, you can get them made with 100% agave tequila.

Of course, it's not only about the booze. There are great nonalcoholic drinks in Austin too, from aguas frescas to great fresh juices and smoothies. Like most things in life, it's all about balance.

And the occasional top-shelf margarita.

Mexican Martini

Mexican Martinis are arguably the only cocktail Austin can truly call its own, and variations on Mexican Martinis are served in Tex-Mex restaurants all over town. In most cases, restaurants guard their recipes closer than state secrets, but luckily for you, I've done my time as a Tex-Mex waitress.

In my experience, a Mexican Martini is just a double margarita with olive brine and vermouth, served in a martini glass with a toothpick full of olives. Some places add a bit of orange juice, but I think it makes the drink look muddy. Your call.

Makes 2 cocktails, or serves 1 person twice.

3 ounces (90 ml) 100% agave tequila

2 ounces (60 ml) fresh lime juice

1½ ounces (45 ml) orange liqueur of your choice

½ ounce (15 ml) olive brine

½ ounce (15 ml) dry vermouth

⅓ ounce (10 ml) fresh orange juice (optional)

Shake all the ingredients with ice. Serve the cocktail in the shaker, with a salt-rimmed martini glass on the side, garnished with a toothpick full of olives. Let guests do the pouring themselves.

Frozen Margaritas

Frozen margaritas have a reputation for being kind of, well, lame, thanks to their sweetness. A purist would most likely order a margarita on the rocks. But a well-made frozen margarita is not only a thing of beauty, it's a necessary component of surviving those 100-degree days we get down here. And if you're going to be snobby about that, fine. More frozen margaritas for me.

Makes 1 pitcher of margaritas, serves 4.

¾ cup (180 ml) 100% agave tequila

½ cup (120 ml) orange liqueur

½ cup (120 ml) fresh lime juice

¼ cup (60 ml) simple syrup
  (see Note, page 186)

Ice

Salt and lime wedges for serving

Pour the tequila, orange liqueur, and lime juice into a blender over about 3 cups (720 ml) ice. Blend until smooth. Serve in salt-rimmed glasses with a wedge of lime.

A Margarita Lexicon

Rocks or frozen? Salt or no? These are the basic questions you'll get when you order a margarita at a restaurant. But the options don't stop there. Here's a guide to all the glorious and varied ways one might order a margarita. You won't see all of these options on every menu, but it sure would be fun if you did.

Beergarita Sometimes called a Solarita or a Coronarita, this is a frozen margarita with a miniature bottle of beer upended into it. As you drink it, the beer mixes with the margarita.

Dot Ordered with a frozen margarita, a dot is a small amount of flavored margarita added to the top of your drink. Good for mixing flavors (strawberry and lime is classic), or for when you don't really want to commit.

En Fuego At Matt's El Rancho, they'll muddle your margarita with sliced jalapeños when you order it "en fuego." (I highly recommend this.)

Flavored Flavors you might see include strawberry, sangria, prickly pear, mango, peach, tamarind, hibiscus, raspberry, cherry, coconut, grapefruit, watermelon, and avocado. Avocado margaritas are a specialty at Curra's, but I've seen them pop up elsewhere recently. And word to the wise: if you order the blue one, you've gone too far.

Floater A shot of something poured over the top of your margarita, so it floats on the surface. Often Grand Marnier or Cointreau or other orange liqueurs, or even a spicy liqueur like Ancho Reyes. (This is often a server's upsell on a top-shelf margarita.)

Frozen Blended with ice. Classic.

House This is a nicer way of describing a margarita made with well liquor. Almost every Tex-Mex place will serve you a house margarita, even if it's not on the menu. Just ask.

Rim Seasoning on the rim of the glass. Typically coated with lime juice and then salted, but sometimes rims feature sugar or salt flavored with spices like chile or cinnamon, or citrus zest.

Rocks Served over ice. Also classic.

Swirl A frozen margarita with a swirl of a second flavor. Halfway between a regular flavored margarita and a dot margarita.

Up Shaken with ice, then strained and served without ice.

Fresh Lime Margaritas

Fonda San Miguel

As top shelf as it gets. Find a good silver tequila you like, and have ingredients for these on hand at all times.

Makes 4 cocktails.

5 lime wedges

Coarse salt

1 cup (240 ml) silver tequila

½ cup (120 ml) Cointreau

½ cup (120 ml) fresh lime juice

Rub the rims of four glasses with a lime wedge. Pour salt into a saucer or shallow dish, then dip each glass into the salt. Set aside.

Shake the tequila, Cointreau, and lime juice with ice until thoroughly chilled, about 30 seconds, then strain into the glasses over fresh ice and garnish with the remaining lime wedges.

OH, BARTENDER?

MY MARGARITA COMBOS OF CHOICE

If it's divey Tex-Mex, I get a strawberry frozen. The strawberry flavor (sometimes made from blended frozen strawberries) will cover the taste of the premade margarita mix. If it's middling Tex-Mex, I order a house margarita, rocks or frozen depending on my mood. If it's a nice place, I order a middle-shelf (not top, not well, but a nice tequila) rocks margarita with a floater of Ancho Reyes. Oh, and salt. Always with salt.

Cucurbit

Contigo

Austin native Nicole Cruz created this cocktail for Contigo, inspired by the "Mexican lollipops, much-coveted at my elementary school" comprised of watermelon candy under a layer of chile. While this cocktail doesn't actually contain watermelon, Cruz explains, "Aperol and gin are natural allies, as are gin and cucumber. Put the three together and they are greater than the sum of their parts. Oddly enough, the combo tastes like watermelon; hence the name: "Cucurbit is a botanical family that counts both watermelon and cucumber among its ranks."

Makes 1 cocktail.

Chile salt, such as Tajín

1 lime wedge

6 slices cucumber

1½ ounces (45 ml) gin

¾ ounce (23 ml) Aperol

½ ounce (15 ml) fresh lime juice

¼ ounce (7.5 ml) simple syrup (see Note)

Pour some chile salt into a shallow dish. Wet the rim of a rocks glass with the lime wedge, then dip it into the dish to coat the rim.

Put 3 of the cucumber slices in a shaker and use a muddler to bash them up a bit. Add the gin, Aperol, lime juice, simple syrup, and a large handful of ice, and shake. Strain into the chile salt–rimmed glasses over fresh ice. Garnish with additional cucumber slices dipped in chile salt.

<u>Note</u>: Simple syrup is a common cocktail ingredient that's super easy to make. Simply heat equal parts sugar and water together in a saucepan until the sugar is dissolved, then allow to cool before using.

Horchata

Tacodeli

Horchata is one of the more common flavors of aguas frescas, the famous Mexican flavored water drinks. Contrary to popular opinion, horchatas are often made without dairy, rendering them vegan. Tacodeli makes theirs from scratch using rice, almonds, cinnamon, vanilla, and evaporated cane juice for a beverage that one young taste tester dubbed "that new drink I love." Try it, you will probably love it too.

Makes 1 pitcher of horchata, serves 4–6.

- ¾ cup (135 g) uncooked basmati or jasmine rice
- 1½ cups (160 g) slivered blanched almonds
- ½ teaspoon ground cinnamon
- ½ teaspoon vanilla paste (not extract)
- ¾ cup (180 ml) evaporated cane juice (or sugar)

Put the rice, almonds, and cinnamon in a pitcher and cover with 6 cups (1.4 L) water. Give it a stir and let soak, covered, at room temperature overnight.

The next day, pour the contents of the pitcher into a blender and add the vanilla paste and evaporated cane juice. Blend thoroughly. Strain the mixture through a cheesecloth-lined mesh strainer. There will be a lot of leftover sediment; you might want to periodically squeeze the excess liquid out of it and dispose of the solids. Do not skip this step, though, or your horchata will be gritty.

Serve over ice.

Colorado Bulldog

For Dorothy

Makes 1 cocktail.

- 1 ounce (30 ml) vodka
- 1 ounce (30 ml) coffee-flavored liqueur
- 1 ounce (30 ml) heavy cream
- Cola

Shake the vodka, coffee liqueur, and cream with ice. Strain into a tall tulip-shaped glass over fresh ice. Top with cola and serve, preferably with a straw.

Cactus Jack Cocktail

Jack Allen's Kitchen

————— ✳ —————

This drink is shockingly, electrically, wonderfully magenta. Blend fresh peeled prickly pears for this if you can find them, but if not you can buy the puree online.

Makes 1 cocktail.

1 tablespoon coarse salt

1 tablespoon chile powder

1 tablespoon grated lime zest

1 lime wedge

1¼ ounces (38 ml) blanco tequila

¾ ounce (23 ml) lemon liqueur

1 ounce (30 ml) simple syrup
(see Note page 186)

1 ounce (30 ml) fresh lime juice

1 tablespoon prickly pear juice
or puree

3 jalapeño slices, with their seeds

Mix the salt, chile powder, and lime zest in a shallow bowl or plate. Use a wedge of lime to moisten the rim of a glass and dip the rim into the salt mixture. Set aside.

Shake all the remaining ingredients with ice. Strain into the chile-rimmed glass over fresh ice.

Mezcal Old Fashioned

Whisler's

————— ✳ —————

Whisler's is a craft cocktail bar on East Sixth Street with a tiny mezcalería upstairs. This cocktail combines a craft cocktail with mezcal to make a drink that's at once unique and familiar.

Makes 1 cocktail.

2 ounces (60 ml) El Silencio mezcal

½ ounce (15 ml) simple syrup
(see Note page 186) made with
Demerara sugar

4 dashes Angostura bitters

1 (2-inch/5-cm) strip of orange peel

1 Luxardo maraschino cherry

Stir the mezcal, simple syrup, and bitters in a cocktail mixer with ice. Stir until cold, about 40 revolutions. Strain into an old fashioned glass over one large fresh ice cube. Rub the orange peel around the rim of the glass, then add to the drink. Add the cherry and serve.

Joanne Cocktail

Odd Duck

Local Texas grapefruits are bright, juicy, and taste amazing. This is a great, simple cocktail from Odd Duck that showcases them.

Makes 1 cocktail.

1½ ounces (45 ml) grapefruit vodka (recipe follows)

¾ ounce (23 ml) ginger liqueur

½ ounce (15 ml) simple syrup (see Note page 186)

½ ounce (15 ml) fresh grapefruit juice

Grapefruit peel

Shake the vodka, ginger liqueur, simple syrup, and grapefruit juice with ice. Strain into an old fashioned glass over fresh ice and garnish with the grapefruit peel.

Grapefruit Vodka

Makes 1 liter.

2 large or 3 small red-fleshed grapefruit, ideally from Texas

½ cup (100 g) sugar

4½ cups (1 liter) vodka

2 big sprigs fresh mint

1 tablespoon pink peppercorns

Peel the grapefruit, removing as much of the bitter white pith as possible. Separate the sections and put the flesh into a gallon-size (3.8-L-size) resealable plastic bag along with the sugar. Mix together and let it sit for 30 minutes or so.

Set the bag in a large bowl (in case it leaks). To the bag add the vodka, mint, and peppercorns. Let it sit at room temperature overnight. Strain the infused vodka through cheesecloth or a coffee filter before serving. The infused vodka can be stored at room temperature in a sealed jar or bottle indefinitely.

Wundershowzen Smoothie

JuiceLand

In Austin, JuiceLand is the place to get juices and smoothies. What started on Barton Springs Road has spread across the city, with locations in Houston, Dallas, and even Brooklyn now. The good people at JuiceLand recommend playing around with the amount of banana to get the right consistency, but however you make it, this smoothie should be nice and thick.

Makes 1 smoothie.

1¼ cups (300 ml) almond milk

1 banana, frozen

⅓ cup (50 g) spinach leaves

2 teaspoons peanut butter

1 tablespoon hemp protein powder

Put all the ingredients in a high-speed blender and blend until smooth.

CHAPTER

BAKED GOODS AND SWEETS

Sweet on Austin

Austin's got the baking bug, no doubt. From pies to cookies to biscuits, sweet or savory, we've never met a carb we didn't adore.

The filled, sweet, yeast dough pastries called *kolache* are an institution throughout Texas, where small-town bakeries just off the highway are necessary road trip pit stops. Although they were brought to the area by Czech immigrants, Texas kolache have really evolved into something entirely different from the European pastry that inspired them.

Along with their meatier twin sibling klobasniki, Texan kolache are available in flavors from the more traditional prune and poppyseed to modern versions like pineapple and strawberry cream cheese. Similarly, you can find klobasniki in flavors from sausage and sauerkraut to jalapeño popper and barbecue. Bakeries in Austin have more recently begun experimenting with kolache flavorings, pulling in inspiration from all over. Which is how we ended up with pastry chef Amanda Rockman's Everything Bagel Kolache (page 203).

There is also a deep pie tradition across this state, where everyone's grandmother inevitably makes the best pie you've ever had. These pies have much in common with the pies of the rest of the South, but they incorporate the state's plentiful native pecans as well as Texas fruits like grapefruits, strawberries, and peaches.

Of course, as always, many of the restaurants in town play with these traditions in their own innovative ways. This chapter explores Austin's baking traditions from the super old-school, like buttermilk pie and cheddar biscuits, to playful, modern treats, including decadent scones that make the most of Texas citrus, and just possibly the best chocolate chip cookies you've ever had.

Pumpkin Bread

Kerbey Lane

This super-moist loaf is used in the Kerbey Lane French toast (page 171), but it's also good on its own. It gets its moisture from the pumpkin puree, in addition to the restaurant's trick of letting the bread cool while covered with foil.

Makes 1 9 by 5 by 2½-inch (23 by 13 by 6-cm) loaf.

1¾ cups (225 g) all-purpose flour

1 teaspoon baking soda

¼ teaspoon baking powder

½ teaspoon salt

¾ teaspoon ground cinnamon

¾ teaspoon grated nutmeg

¼ teaspoon ground cloves

1 can (15 ounces/425 g) pumpkin puree

2 large eggs

1½ cups (300 g) sugar

½ cup (120 ml) vegetable oil

Heat the oven to 350°F (175°C).

Whisk together the flour, baking soda, baking powder, salt, cinnamon, nutmeg, and cloves in a mixing bowl. In a separate, larger bowl, whisk together the pumpkin puree, eggs, sugar, and oil until smooth. Add the dry mixture to the wet mixture and whisk until the lumps disappear, stopping to scrape the sides of the bowl a couple times with a spatula.

Pour the batter into a greased 9 by 5-inch (23 by 13-cm) loaf pan and set the pan on a sheet pan. Bake until a toothpick inserted in the center comes out clean, about 1 hour. Let the bread cool for 10 minutes, then cover the loaf pan with foil until the bread is completely cooled. (This helps to ensure a moist loaf.) Serve, either as French toast (page 171) or on its own.

Cheddar Biscuits

Frank

Honestly, is there anything better than a fresh-from-the-oven biscuit? These incorporate shredded cheddar as part of the fat in the dough, which makes for a flaky, savory biscuit. Use these in the Texas Benedict (page 169) or on their own for breakfast. They're quick to whip up; the key is to keep your ingredients cold and not overmix the dough.

Makes 8 large biscuits.

4 cups (510 g) all-purpose flour

4 teaspoons granulated garlic powder

2 tablespoons baking powder

½ teaspoon baking soda

4 teaspoons salt

4 tablespoons (55 g) unsalted butter, frozen, plus 2 tablespoons melted

2 cups (200 g) shredded cheddar cheese

2 cups (480 ml) buttermilk, chilled

Heat the oven to 350°F (175°C).

Put the flour, garlic powder, baking powder, baking soda, and salt in a food processor and pulse briefly to combine. Slice the frozen butter and add it to the food processor along with the cheese and pulse until the mixture is clumpy. (Don't overdo it.)

Transfer the flour and cheese mixture to a large mixing bowl. Slowly—bit by bit—add the buttermilk, folding it with a spatula until you get a ball of dough. Press the dough out on a floured surface with your fingers to make a large rectangle that's about ½ inch (12 mm) thick (do not use a rolling pin!). Fold the dough over itself three times (like you're folding a pamphlet or a letter). Cut the biscuits using a large circular biscuit cutter, taking care to press the cutter straight down and not twist it. You can rework the excess dough or just bake the scraps alongside the biscuits.

Bake the biscuits on a parchment-lined sheet pan for 20 to 25 minutes, until flaky and lightly golden brown on top. Brush the tops with melted butter and serve.

Bootsie's Buttermilk Pie

Eastside Cafe

Today Manor Road is packed with restaurants, but Eastside Cafe has been serving seasonal treats on that stretch since 1988.

This luscious buttermilk pie is one of their signature dishes, best enjoyed topped with peak-season strawberries. (Which, in Texas, means spring.) The restaurant bakes this pie in its own signature oval pie plates, but a deep-dish pan works just as well.

Makes 1 9-inch (23-cm) deep-dish pie.
(This will work in a non-deep-dish pan, but you will have some filling left over.)

For the crust

1½ cups (190 g) all-purpose flour

1 tablespoon sugar

½ teaspoon salt

½ cup (120 ml) canola oil

1 tablespoon milk

For the filling

½ cup (1 stick/115 g) unsalted butter, cut into cubes

2 cups (400 g) sugar

2 large eggs

1 cup (240 ml) buttermilk

¼ cup (30 g) all-purpose flour

1 tablespoon vanilla extract

To serve

1 pint (290 g) fresh strawberries

1 teaspoon sugar

Make the crust: Combine the flour, sugar, and salt in a mixing bowl. Add the oil and milk, and stir just until combined. Using your hands, form the dough into a ball. Press the dough into the bottom and sides of a 9-inch (23 cm) deep-dish pie pan using your fingers, keeping the dough as evenly distributed as possible. Prick the dough all over with a fork and refrigerate for at least 30 minutes.

Heat the oven to 350°F (175°C). Line the pie crust with a sheet of foil, then fill the foil with pie weights (or dried beans). Bake for 15 minutes. Remove the partially baked crust from the oven, remove the pie weights and foil, and let cool completely. Lower the oven temperature to 325°F.

Make the filling: In a stand mixer fitted with a paddle attachment, cream the butter and sugar together at medium speed until the color lightens, about 5 minutes. Add the eggs one at a time, mixing until fully incorporated. Add the buttermilk, flour, and vanilla and mix for about 2 minutes. The mixture might curdle a little when you add the buttermilk—don't worry, it should come back together somewhat as you mix it, and it will come together completely when it bakes.

Pour the batter into the crust and bake for 50 minutes. The filling should be ever-so-slightly jiggly in the middle when it is done. Let cool completely.

Hull and slice the strawberries and place them in a bowl. Toss the berries with the sugar and let them sit for about 5 minutes, then serve slices of pie topped with the sliced strawberries.

Everything Bagel Kolache

Mañana

Inspired by New York flavors, these innovative kolache are nevertheless very Texan: yeasty and sweet and soft and full of gooey filling. Pastry chef Amanda Rockman, who grew up in Texas, says the idea for these came from her family: "My father is from the Bronx and we are also Jewish, so the idea of bagels and cream cheese is second nature to my family."

Of course, if you are a fan of sweeter kolache, you could fill this dough with your favorite jam or other sugary fillings. To make klobasniki, wrap it around small smoked sausages like kielbasa (page 29). This dough won't rise dramatically (like bread might), but I promise the end result will be large, fluffy, pillowy kolache.

Start these the day before you plan to bake them, as the dough needs to rest in the refrigerator overnight.

Makes 12 kolache.

1½ cups (360 ml) whole milk

4 teaspoons active dry yeast

½ cup (100 g) sugar

5 cups (640 g) all-purpose flour

3 large eggs

4½ tablespoons (65 g) unsalted butter, melted and cooled, plus an additional 4 tablespoons (55 g) melted butter to brush the dough

3 teaspoons kosher salt

Cream cheese filling (recipe follows)

Everything bagel topping (recipe follows)

RECIPE CONTINUES ⟶

Heat the milk until warm but not hot in a small saucepan (or use the microwave). In a medium mixing bowl, combine the warm milk, yeast, sugar, and 2 cups (255 g) of the flour, being careful not to overmix. Cover the bowl with plastic and let it sit for about 15 minutes, until the mixture is doubled in size.

Meanwhile, in a stand mixer fitted with the whisk attachment, beat the eggs, 4½ tablespoons (65 g) melted butter, and salt together briefly. Add the risen yeast mixture and stir to combine. Attach the dough hook and slowly add the remaining 3 cups (385 g) flour, then knead the mixture on medium-low speed until shiny and elastic, about 10 minutes.

Place the dough in a greased bowl and cover with plastic. Refrigerate overnight.

The next day, divide the dough into 12 equal portions. Shape into balls and place them on a greased sheet pan. Use your hand to flatten the balls slightly, so they're about 3 inches (7.5 cm) in diameter. Brush the kolache rounds with some of the remaining 4 tablespoons (55 g) melted butter, cover them with a kitchen towel, and let them rise for 45 minutes.

Heat the oven to 375°F (190°C).

Use your thumb to make an indentation the size of each scoop of filling on top of every risen round. Place 1 scoop of the cream cheese mixture in each indentation, then sprinkle each kolache with 1 teaspoon everything bagel topping. (You'll have some topping leftover.) Bake for about 18 minutes, until the dough is golden brown. Remove the kolache from the oven and brush them with any leftover melted butter, then serve warm.

Cream Cheese Filling

8 ounces (225 g) cream cheese, at
room temperature

1 teaspoon sugar

½ teaspoon salt

2 tablespoons thinly sliced fresh
chives

In a stand mixer, whisk the cream
cheese with the sugar and salt until
light and fluffy, about 5 minutes—the
cream cheese should increase in
volume as air is incorporated into
the cheese. Fold in the chives. Form
1-tablespoon balls of the mixture and
place them on a sheet pan lined with
waxed or parchment paper. Press the
tops of each balls with the back of
a spoon to flatten them slightly into
discs, then freeze overnight. (You'll
put them on the kolache dough frozen
before baking.)

Everything Bagel Topping

¾ teaspoon salt

1 tablespoon white sesame seeds

2 teaspoons black sesame seeds

2 teaspoons poppy seeds

1 tablespoon dried onion

1 teaspoon dried onion powder

½ teaspoon granulated garlic
powder

Combine all the ingredients in a small
bowl. Extra topping can be stored in
an airtight container.

Pecan Pie

Cutie Pie Wagon

National champion pie baker Jaynie Buckingham serves this pecan pie out of her bright pink pie trailer, the Cutie Pie Wagon. Her version of this iconic pie gets a double hit of the native Texas nuts, incorporating pecan pieces as well as a handful of pecan cookies crumbled into the filling for a unique and tasty texture. Buckingham also adds just a hint of honey, making for a truly spectacular upgrade on the classic.

Makes 1 (9-inch/23-cm) pie.

For the crust

1½ cups (190 g) all-purpose flour

½ cup (1 stick/115 g) cold unsalted butter, cut into pieces

¼ cup (60 ml) ice cold water

Make the crust: Put the flour in a bowl. Using a pastry cutter or two forks, work the cold butter into the flour until the butter is in pea-size pieces. Gradually work in the cold water until the dough just barely comes together. Knead the dough a few times, taking care not to overwork it. Form the dough into a ball, wrap it with plastic, and flatten the ball slightly to form a disc. Chill the dough for 30 minutes in the refrigerator.

Heat the oven to 350°F (175°C).

Roll out the dough until it's large enough to line a 9-inch (23-cm) pie pan. Settle the dough into the pan and crimp the edges with a fork or with your fingers. Line the dough with foil and fill the foil with pie weights (or dried beans). Bake the crust until it is set but still blond, about 6 minutes. Remove the pie weights and foil.

For the filling

¾ cup (165 g) brown sugar

¾ cup (180 ml) light corn syrup

4 large eggs

½ cup (50 g) crumbled store-bought pecan cookies

½ cup (60 g) pecan pieces

½ cup (1 stick/115 g) unsalted butter, melted and cooled

2 tablespoons honey

Make the filling: In a large bowl, combine all the ingredients for the filling until incorporated. Pour the filling into the prepared crust and bake for 30 to 35 minutes. You want the pie filling to have a very slight wobble, just in the center, when it is finished. Let the pie cool completely before serving.

Salted Brown Butter and Dark Chocolate Pecan Cookies

Lenoir

This is the only recipe in this book by someone who works front of house: Emmy Hangartner, the manager at Lenoir. You'd never know these amazing cookies weren't the work of a pastry chef, though. Layers upon layers of flavor—from browned butter to dark chocolate to toasted pecans to the smoked maldon salt that finishes everything off—add up to one incredible cookie.

Makes about 24 cookies.

1 cup (2 sticks/225 g) unsalted butter

3 large eggs, at room temperature

2 teaspoons vanilla extract

3 cups (385 g) all-purpose flour

½ teaspoon kosher salt

½ teaspoon cream of tartar

1 cup (200 g) granulated sugar

1 cup (220 g) packed light brown sugar

1 teaspoon baking soda

2 teaspoons hot water

2 cups (200 g) pecans, toasted and roughly chopped

8 ounces (225 g) high-quality dark chocolate (60 to 75% cocoa), roughly chopped to chocolate chip–sized pieces

Smoked Maldon salt

Melt the butter in a small saucepan over medium heat. It will foam and die down, and then foam again. After the second foam, you'll start to smell a distinct nuttiness; the butter will be a light tan color. Pour the browned butter into a heat-resistant container and then put it in the refrigerator to cool. Remove the butter when it has returned to the consistency of softened butter, about 1 hour 30 minutes, depending on how cold your refrigerator is.

Heat the oven to 350°F (175°C).

In a small bowl, briefly whisk together the eggs and vanilla and set aside. In another bowl, sift together the flour, kosher salt, and cream of tartar and set aside.

RECIPE CONTINUES ⟶

In a stand mixer fitted with the paddle attachment, beat the brown butter briefly, 15 to 20 seconds, then add the sugars and beat until light and fluffy, 3 to 4 minutes.

Add half of the egg and vanilla mixture to the butter mixture and mix to combine. Add the second half and mix to combine. Scrape the sides of the bowl with a spatula, then mix for another 30 seconds to bring it all together.

Dissolve the baking soda in the hot water. Add this to the butter mixture and mix for another 10 seconds. Remove the bowl from the stand mixer. Add the flour mixture all at once and bring the dough together, stirring by hand. Add the pecans and choco-late, again stirring by hand.

Drop large spoonfuls of the dough—2 to 3 tablespoons' worth each—on a parchment-lined baking sheet, leaving about 2 inches (5 cm) between the cookies. Flatten the top of each cookie slightly. Bake for 8 minutes. Rotate the baking sheet 180 degrees, then bake another 5 to 6 minutes, until the edges are just starting to brown.

Remove from the oven and let the cookies cool on the baking sheet for a couple minutes, then sprinkle lightly with the smoked salt. Transfer the cookies to a wire rack and let cool completely.

Daniel Vaughn's Banana Pudding

If you still have room after stuffing your face with barbecue, order the banana pudding. Often made with artificially flavored pudding mix, this old-fashioned dessert can get a bad rap. But if you make the pudding from scratch, like *Texas Monthly* Barbecue Editor Daniel Vaughn does, you'll discover that this creamy pudding is a delicious treat.

Vaughn says, "Homemade vanilla wafers are great, but Nilla wafers work just fine, and the smaller ones make for an easier spoonful. Skip any and all frozen whipped topping."

Serves 6–8, loosely fills a 13 by 9-inch (33 by 23-cm) baking dish.

6 just-ripe bananas (you want the interior to be pale yellow, with no brown spots)

2 tablespoons fresh lemon juice

1 quart (960 ml) half-and-half

4 large egg yolks

⅓ cup (40 g) all-purpose flour

½ cup (100 g) sugar

1 teaspoon salt

⅓ cup (75 ml) sour cream

2 teaspoons vanilla extract

½ box (5½ ounces/155 g) Nilla wafers

Quarter 2 of the bananas and micro-wave them for 45 to 60 seconds, until very soft. In a medium bowl, use a fork to mash them with the lemon juice. Whisk the half-and-half and egg yolks into the bananas.

Bring an inch (2.5 cm) of water to a boil in a medium saucepan. Set a heatproof metal or glass bowl in the pan so it touches the water but not the bottom of the pan to set up a double boiler. Add the flour, sugar, and salt to the bowl and stir to combine. Add the half-and-half mixture and whisk continuously for 7 to 10 minutes until it thickens to the consistency of cake batter. Remove the bowl from the pan.

Combine the sour cream and vanilla with the pudding mixture. Let cool to room temperature, about 1 hour. If you prefer mushy wafers—and some people do—skip the cooling step here and build the pudding.

Cut the 4 remaining bananas into slices ½ inch (12 mm) thick. Arrange one-third of the Nilla wafers in the bottom of a large shallow serving dish. Layer half of the bananas over the wafers. Pour half of the pudding mixture over the wafers and bananas. Add another layer with one-third of the wafers and the remaining bananas. Pour the remaining pudding over the bananas and top with a layer of the remaining Nilla wafers. Chill in the refrigerator for several hours (or overnight) until completely cool before serving.

Texas Citrus Scones

Emmer & Rye

Grapefruit isn't the only citrus that grows in Texas. Pastry chef Tavel Bristol-Joseph uses Texas oranges for the marmalade in these scones for their sweetness, but you can vary the dried fruit and citrus zest to your liking. This recipe produces a sweet, rich scone that is light-years beyond the dry, crumbly pastry of common imagination.

Makes about 24–32 scones.

5 cups (625 g) pastry or cake flour

1 teaspoon salt

1¼ cups (250 g) sugar

2 tablespoons baking powder

⅓ cup (50 g) chopped dried fruit (raisins, apricots, cranberries—your pick)

Grated zest of ½ orange (or grapefruit or other citrus)

4 tablespoons (55 g) cold butter, cut into small cubes

2 large eggs

1⅓ cups (315 ml) plus ½ cup (120 ml) heavy cream

¾ cup (180 ml) orange marmalade

In the bowl of a stand mixer fitted with the paddle attachment, combine the flour, salt, ¼ cup (50 g) of the sugar, the baking powder, dried fruit, and zest.

Remove the bowl from the stand mixer. Add the butter to the flour mixture and use a pastry knife or a fork to cut the butter into the flour, until the mixture becomes mealy.

Put the bowl back on the mixer and attach the paddle. Add the eggs and mix until combined, then add the 1⅓ cups (315 ml) cream and the marmalade and mix until combined.

Use a scoop to portion out the dough into ¼- to ⅓-cup (60- to 75-ml) balls and place them on a parchment paper–lined baking sheet. Refrigerate until chilled through, about 2 hours. (If you don't chill the scones thoroughly, they won't bake properly.)

Heat the oven to 350°F (175°C).

Combine the remaining 1 cup (200 g) sugar with just enough of the remaining ½ cup (120 ml) cream to moisten it to the consistency of very wet sand. Spread about 1 teaspoon of the mixture on top of each scone. This will create a crunchy topping while baking.

Bake for 25 minutes, or until golden brown on top.

CHAPTER

9

SALSAS, SAUCES, AND CHILIS

Some Like It (Very) Hot

Salsa can make or break a taco. The best braised meats or migas won't sing if they're doused in a flabby sauce. Same with enchiladas. Same with eggs. Same with—well, you get the idea. Salsas can be anything from the super simple to the incredibly complex. And just like any other Mexican-influenced dish served around here, Austin's salsas draw on both interior Mexican and local traditions.

Most of these salsas are paired with specific dishes elsewhere in the book, but feel free to mix and match according to your preference. Or, heck, serve them alone with chips. Watch out, though, there are some spicy ones in here.

That said, the spiciness of your salsas may vary greatly. The heat level of chiles can change depending on the time of year, the weather where they were grown, the length of time they were left on the plant before harvest, and how long they've been stored. I've noted which salsas have a tendency to be particularly spicy, but you may have entirely different results than I did. A good rule: if you're sensitive to heat, remove the seeds and veins from any chiles you use.

Chilis are included in this chapter, because technically chili is a sauce (at least in Texas). Both of the chili recipes in this chapter can be served over other dishes (enchiladas, Frito pie) or on their own, or with chips or saltines or cornbread. I can say with confidence that both of these recipes are pretty spicy, since the heat level of dried chiles and chile powder is more consistent. (That said, dried chiles and chile powder can go stale, so don't keep them around forever.)

Pico de Gallo

This salsa is about as simple as it gets, so it helps to use the absolute best ingredients you can get your hands on. That means, ideally, ripe, in-season tomatoes. You can eat this with just about anything, and customize it to be as spicy or as tame as you'd like.

Makes about 2 cups (480 ml) salsa.

2 ripe tomatoes, diced

½ white onion, diced

1 jalapeño, minced

1 handful fresh cilantro, roughly chopped

Salt

Fresh lime juice

Combine the tomatoes, onion, jalapeño, and cilantro in a small bowl, then add salt and lime juice to taste. It will taste better if you let it sit and come together at room temperature for 30 minutes or so before serving.

Vegan Lentil Chili

Texas Chili Queens

The name of the Texas Chili Queens food truck has a double meaning. First, it's an homage to the original, nineteenth-century chili slingers, the Texas Chili Queens of San Antonio. Second, it is staffed by Edie Eclat, the retro Betty Crocker–in–a–wig drag queen persona of owner Ed Hambleton. "The drag is a way to reinterpret what a chili queen is," says Hambleton. "We keep Austin weird while serving a quintessential dish."

Lentils make for a brilliant vegetarian substitute for meat in a Texas-style chili. They replicate the texture of the traditional coarse-ground beef and manage to get around the most common vegetarian chili ingredient: beans.

(Don't tell the Chili Queens I told you this, but this is also excellent with cooked ground beef instead of or in addition to the lentils.)

Serves 8 to 10.

3 ounces (85 g) dried guajillo chiles

3 ounces (85 g) dried New Mexico (Anaheim) chiles

2 heaping cups (220 g) brown lentils

⅓ cup (35 g) paprika

4 teaspoons cumin

4 teaspoons black pepper

4 teaspoons onion powder

2 teaspoons granulated garlic powder

⅓ cup chili (40 g) powder

4 teaspoons celery salt

2 cans (28 ounces/794 g each) diced tomatoes with their liquid

Salt

Remove the seeds and stems from the dried chiles and put them in a heat-safe glass container. Cover with boiling water and set aside for about 30 minutes. Once cooled, put the chiles and their soaking liquid in a blender or food processor. Puree until smooth; the mixture should be thick, but pourable. If you've got some serious sludge on your hands, add a bit more water.

Put the lentils, chile puree, 4 cups (960 ml) water, the paprika, cumin, black pepper, onion powder, and garlic powder in a large pot over medium-high heat. Cover and simmer until most of the liquid is absorbed, about 2 hours, stirring frequently to make sure the lentils don't stick to the bottom of the pot and scorch.

Add the chili powder, celery salt, and tomatoes. Stir and continue cooking until the lentils are cooked through and tender, about 2 more hours. Season with salt and serve.

JAK's Salsa

Jack Allen's Kitchen

A half-step more complex than pico, you can find cooked red salsas all over the place—although, of course, everyone has their own version of it. This one, from Jack Allen's Kitchen, is combined with cream for the sauce on their Enchiladas Tejanas (page 88), although it's also great on its own with chips.

Makes about 4 cups (960 ml) salsa.

6 small tomatoes, such as Roma

4 tomatillos, husked

4 dried guajillo chiles, stems removed

½ cup (55 g) chopped onion

4 garlic cloves, chopped

2 teaspoons onion salt

Heat the broiler to high. Put the tomatoes and tomatillos on a sheet pan and broil until the skin blisters, making sure they don't burn.

In a medium pot, bring the tomatoes, tomatillos, chiles, onion, and 2 cups water to a boil. Lower the heat and simmer for 10 minutes. Let cool.

Blend the tomato mixture, garlic, and onion salt in a blender or food processor until slightly chunky. Season to taste. Store, covered, in the refrigerator, for up to a week.

Salsa de la Casa

El Alma Cafe

Chef Alma Alcocer-Thomas makes several wickedly good sauces, but this roasty number from her namesake restaurant is a standout. The pickled jalapeños add a nice spicy-sour note, while the dried chiles give it a deeper flavor and darker color than the JAK Salsa.

Makes about 2 cups (480 ml) salsa.

½ ounce (14 g) dried chiles of your choice, such as moritas or arbol, stems removed

1 pound (455 g) Roma tomatoes

6 garlic cloves, peeled and left whole

1 teaspoon kosher salt, or more to taste

½ cup (80 g) pickled jalapeños with their brine (page 226 or store-bought)

1 teaspoon dried oregano

Toast the dried chiles briefly in a dry skillet, until you can smell them, about 1 minute. Put them in a heatproof bowl, cover with very hot water, and set aside.

Heat the broiler to high. Place the tomatoes on a sheet pan and broil until the skin is charred. Remove some of the skin (but not all of it—some char is nice!) and set the tomatoes aside to cool. Broil the garlic just slightly as well, until black in spots and aromatic.

Drain the dried chiles. In a molcajete (or a food processor if you don't have one), crush the garlic with the drained chiles and salt until a smooth paste is formed. Add the tomatoes, jalapeños and their brine, and oregano and crush until smooth. Season with more salt if you like.

Salsa Macha Verde

Veracruz All-Natural

Just as often as you hear the question "Corn or flour?" you'll hear "Red or green?" This is the green option at famed taco truck Veracruz All-Natural. Make a big batch and slather it over their breakfast tacos (page 159). And be careful, this one can be very hot.

Makes about ½ cup (120 ml) salsa.

6 large jalapeños

2 garlic cloves

Salt

Juice of 1 large lime

Grill the jalapeños over high heat briefly, until they form grill marks, or toast them in a hot cast-iron pan over high heat until blackened in spots. Remove the stems and put the jalapeños in a food processor.

Add the garlic, a couple pinches of salt, 1 tablespoon water, and the lime juice and process until completely blended. Add more salt if needed.

THE GREEN SAUCE

I know of no other salsa that inspires so many blissed-out eye rolls than the infamous green sauce served at taquerias across Austin. In many ways it inspires such devotion because it's sort of a mystery. The only thing most people know is that it's hot, it's creamy, and it sort of seems like it has avocado in it.

It doesn't. This type of salsa typically gets its creaminess from pureeing green chiles and garlic with oil, which results in a creamy salsa that, yes, sort of mimics the effect of avocado. Emulsified sauces like this are actually pretty common throughout Texas and Latin America—Peruvian cuisine is full of them, for example. This particular type of green emulsified salsa is popular enough throughout Austin that the supermarket chain HEB bottles its own version called, simply, That Green Sauce. No introductions necessary.

To make your own creamy green sauce at home, start with a simple green salsa like the Salsa Macha Verde (page 223) or, honestly, you could make it with something store-bought.

Puree the salsa in a food processor or blender until it's almost completely smooth, then start slowly drizzling vegetable oil into the salsa while the processor is running. (About 1 cup (240 ml) if you're using the Macha Verde recipe.) Continue adding vegetable oil until you have a creamy salsa that's still a little runny—it should be thinner than mayonnaise.

It's not entirely proper, but I also like to add a handful of cilantro to the mix. Hey, the only way to improve on that green sauce is to make it greener.

Grapefruit Salsa

Swift's Attic

This grapefruit salsa is technically intended for the Braised Pig Tail Puffy Tacos (page 49), but it's also fabulous on its own.

Makes about 1 cup (240 ml) salsa.

2 Texas grapefruits

2 jalapeños, minced

1 small red onion, finely diced (about ½ cup/55 g)

2 sprigs' worth of fresh oregano leaves, chopped

Salt and black pepper

Cut the peel and pith from the grapefruits. Holding the citrus over a bowl to catch the juice, cut the segments of fruit out from between the membranes. (The resulting membrane-free citrus segments are called supremes.) Finely dice the segments.

Mix the diced grapefruit and juice, the jalapeños, onion, and oregano. Add salt and black pepper to taste. Chill for at least 20 minutes to let the flavors develop before serving.

Pickled Jalapeños

Bufalina

This is how Bufalina makes pickled jalapeños for their pizzas, but you can use these on everything from tacos to nachos to Frito pie.

Makes 1 quart (1 L) jar of pickled jalapeños.

1 cup (240 ml) white wine vinegar
½ tablespoon salt
3 garlic cloves, peeled and left whole
1 bay leaf
½ tablespoon black peppercorns
8 ounces (225 g) jalapeños

Put the vinegar, 1 cup (240 ml) water, the salt, garlic, bay leaf, and peppercorns in a medium saucepan over low heat and stir; heat until the salt is dissolved. Let cool.

Prick each jalapeño a few times with a fork or a paring knife and place them in a nonreactive container with a lid. Pour the pickling mixture over the chiles and cover; refrigerate for at least 3 days before using. These will keep for several months, covered, in the refrigerator.

Hot Sauce

Barley Swine

Many types of hot sauce require some type of fermented chile. This one calls for a sweet chile ferment. You use sweet chiles because if you were to use hot chiles like serranos or jalapeños, the end result would turn out way too spicy. This is the essential ingredient in Barley Swine's famous pig skin noodles (page 147).

Makes 2 cups (480 ml) sauce.

Sweet red chile ferment (recipe on following page)

¼ cup (60 ml) banana pepper vinegar

3 tablespoons fresh lime juice

1½ tablespoons honey

2 teaspoons salt

½ teaspoon MSG

3 whole Thai chiles

½ gram xanthan gum (available online)

½ cup (1 stick/115 g) unsalted butter, melted and cooled

Heat all the ingredients except the butter together in a saucepan until hot but not simmering. Carefully pour the heated ingredients and the butter into a blender and blend until smooth. Pour through a strainer set over a bowl, then funnel into a clean jar and store in the refrigerator. Shake vigorously before serving.

Sweet Red Chile Ferment

8 ounces (225 g) sweet red chile peppers
1 teaspoon sugar
Pinch of salt

Remove the seeds and stems from the peppers and place in a food processor. Pulse until the chiles are chopped—it doesn't have to be super fine. Combine the chiles with the sugar and salt and place them in a clean glass container. Cover the glass container loosely with plastic wrap, making sure the chiles can come in contact with air to allow for fermentation. Place in a cabinet or another cool, dark place.

Every day for a week, stir the chiles and replace the cover with clean plastic wrap. As the peppers release liquid, you may need to put weights on top of the plastic to keep the chiles submerged in the liquid—dry beans work well. After a week the peppers should taste good and funky, but you can go a bit longer if you like.

When ready, bring the mixture to a boil briefly, then let cool. Pour the mixture through a strainer set over a bowl and discard the solids. Store in a sealed container in the refrigerator until you make the hot sauce.

CHILI CHAT
∗
NO BEANS ABOUT IT

Texas chili, famously, contentiously, does not have beans. Some recipes are as simple as ground beef and chili powder; others are more complex and full of secret ingredients from beer to cocoa powder to coffee to peanut butter. One ingredient you won't find in Texas chili, though? Beans.*

There are all sorts of explanations for this. Here's one I like from the legendary *Time Life Foods of the World* series—the Texas chapters were written by Jonathan Norton Leonard and published in 1971: "Beans should not intrude on chili con carne. They have muscled their way into the dish only because they are cheaper than meat and because New Yorkers, Chicagoans and the buyers of most kinds of canned chili don't know when they are being imposed on."

In other words, beans were added to cover up the inferior flavor of inferior chilis. Whether or not this is historically accurate, this theory is flattering to Texan recipes and therefore approved.

This is actually, technically, not true. You can in fact find chili in Texas that includes beans, or, perhaps more accurately, you can find chili that is served with beans. Like all things, it's a matter of personal preference and individual restaurant style. But you didn't hear it from me.

Chile con Carne Sauce

Maudie's

This is about as old-school as it gets. This recipe is just ground beef, spices, and water, more or less, but that's all you really need. This goes on the Chile con Carne Enchiladas (page 79).

Makes enough for 12 enchiladas.

8 ounces (225 ml) ground beef

2 tablespoons dark chile powder

2 teaspoons paprika

1½ teaspoons granulated garlic powder

1 teaspoon ground cumin

1 teaspoon black pepper

1½ teaspoons salt

2 tablespoons cornstarch

Put the beef in a pot, add 1 cup (240 ml) water, and stir until thoroughly combined. Bring the mixture to a boil, then lower the heat to a simmer over medium-low heat. Break up the chunks of ground beef with the back of a spoon and simmer until just cooked through, 8 to 10 minutes.

Meanwhile, combine the chile powder, paprika, garlic powder, cumin, black pepper, and salt in a small bowl. Set aside.

Add 2 cups water to the pot and return to a boil. Add the spices, reduce the heat to medium-low, and simmer for 8 to 10 minutes.

In a small bowl, combine the cornstarch with 1 cup (240 ml) cold water and slowly pour the mixture into the chili, stirring. Simmer for 4 more minutes, and the sauce is ready for enchiladas or whatever you see fit to serve it over.

Verde Sauce

This is an enchilada sauce, best served over chicken enchiladas with melted white cheese and a dab of sour cream. It's also good over eggs or layered into nachos.

Makes about 2 quarts (2 L) sauce.

1 quart (1 L) chicken stock or water

Salt

8 tomatillos, husked

6 garlic cloves, peeled and smashed

1 small white onion, cut in half

2 jalapeños, cut in half lengthwise, stems removed

1 large bunch fresh cilantro

In a medium saucepan, bring the stock to a simmer. Add a couple pinches of salt along with the tomatillos, garlic, onion, and jalapeños. Lower the heat to a simmer and cook for 15 minutes. Remove from the heat and let cool.

Once the tomatillo mixture is cool, transfer it to a blender (or use an immersion blender right in the saucepan) along with the cilantro and blend until smooth. Season with salt, reheat, and serve warm.

Ranchero Sauce

Joe's Bakery

This makes for a good vegetarian enchilada sauce, but it really shines on Huevos Rancheros (page 167).

Makes about 2 quarts (2 L) sauce.

1 tablespoon vegetable oil

1 cup (125 g) finely diced onion

1 cup (100 g) finely diced celery

1 cup (145 g) finely diced green bell pepper

1 teaspoon salt

1 teaspoon ground cumin

2 teaspoons granulated garlic powder

1 can (7 ounces/200 g) green chiles or jalapeños, drained and chopped

1 can (14½ ounces/411 g) whole tomatoes

1 can (14½ ounces/411 g) crushed tomatoes

In a medium pot, heat the oil over medium heat. Add the onion, celery, bell pepper, salt, cumin, and garlic powder. Cook, stirring occasionally, until the vegetables are soft, about 10 minutes.

Add the chiles, tomatoes, and two tomato cans' worth of water to the pot. Bring to a boil, then reduce to a simmer. Simmer for 40 minutes, stirring to break up the tomatoes; the mixture should be soupy. This will last in the refrigerator for about a week, and up to two months in the freezer.

FURTHER READING

AFIELD: A CHEF'S GUIDE
TO PREPARING AND COOKING WILD
GAME AND FISH
by Jesse Griffiths

AUSTIN BREAKFAST TACOS:
THE STORY OF THE MOST
IMPORTANT TACO OF THE DAY
by Mando Rayo and Jarrod Neece

COOKING TEXAS STYLE by
Candy Wagner and Sandra Marquez

FONDA SAN MIGUEL: FORTY YEARS
OF FOOD AND ART by
Tom Gilliland and Miguel Ravago

FRANKLIN BARBECUE: A
MEAT-SMOKING MANIFESTO by
Aaron Franklin and Jordan Mackay

THE HOMESICK TEXAN COOKBOOK
by Lisa Fain

JACK ALLEN'S KITCHEN: CELE-
BRATING THE TASTE OF TEXAS by
Jack Gilmore and Jessica Dupuy

LEGENDS OF TEXAS BARBECUE
COOKBOOK by Robb Walsh

MEATHEAD: THE SCIENCE OF
GREAT BARBECUE AND GRILLING
by Meathead Goldwyn and Greg Blonder

THE PROPHETS OF SMOKED MEAT:
A JOURNEY THROUGH TEXAS BAR-
BECUE by Daniel Vaughn

SMOKE: NEW FIREWOOD COOKING
by Tim Byres

SWEET ON TEXAS: LOVABLE CON-
FECTIONS FROM THE LONE STAR
STATE by Denise Gee

TEXAS EATS: THE NEW LONE STAR
HERITAGE COOKBOOK by Robb Walsh

TEXAS ON THE TABLE: PEOPLE,
PLACES, AND RECIPES CELEBRAT-
ING THE FLAVORS OF THE LONE
STAR STATE by Terry Thompson-
Anderson

THE TEX-MEX COOKBOOK: A HIS-
TORY IN RECIPES AND PHOTOS by
Robb Walsh

TIPSY TEXAN: SPIRITS AND COCK-
TAILS FROM THE LONE STAR STATE
by David Alan

UCHI: THE COOKBOOK
by Tyson Cole and Jessica Dupuy

ACKNOWLEDGMENTS

Thanks to: the endlessly generous and terrifically talented Austin restaurant community; photographer to the stars Robert Strickland; my fabulous editor Holly Dolce and everyone at Abrams; my incredible agent Angela Miller; brilliant food stylist and certified native Austinite Liz Pearson; forever Texans Andrea Grimes and Meghan McCarron; the one-and-only Deana Saukam; Mr. Barbecue himself, Daniel Vaughn; the legendary Pat Sharpe; my loving and wonderful parents, Sarah Mason and Barry Forbes; my gorgeous and irreplaceable sister Madeline Forbes; the astoundingly helpful team of recipe testers for this book (Keegan Austin and Dulcie Austin, Rachel Collins and Donovan Gentry, Karen Anderson, Claire Odom, Amy McKeever, Will Grindle, Georgianna "Pancakes" Barker, James Prior, Freeda Brook, Christina Dennehy, Liz Mallott, Jessica Hixson, Mark Bourne, Molly Offer-Westort, Nick DePetris, Adrianne Klein, Christine Remissong, Maurie Kathan, Paul Heider, Dana Roman, Kaitlin Loyal, Sasank Ancha, Molly, Jess Eaton, Sarah Smith, and the entire vibrant Grinnell Plans community); vital cookbook advice pals Matt Rodbard, Kaitlyn Goalen and Katie Parla; the patient and ridiculously helpful staffs of Resplendent Hospitality, Giant Noise, Cultivate PR, Paula Biehler PR, and Brenda Thompson Communications; and, of course, the entire Posse gang. But most of all thank you, thank you, thank you to my love, Raphael Brion. I couldn't have done this without any of you.

INDEX

A

Alcocer-Thomas, Alma, 222
Alcomar, 91–92
almond milk, *192*, 193
Armstrong, Bob, 70, 72
Asazu, Takehiro, 124
Austin, 7–8, 61, 98, 124. *See also*
  East Austin
Avila, Joe, 162
avocado, 52, *53*, 137, 157
  Guacamole, 70, *71*, *74*, 75

B

bacon, 157
  Joe's Bakery, 165, *165*, *166*, 167
  24 Hash, 160, *161*
Baked Oysters, *116*, 117
Bakra Goat Burger, 144, *145*, 146
banana, *192*, 193
  Daniel Vaughn's Banana Pudding, 211
banana leaves, 93
Banh Mi Tacos, *60*, 61–62
barbecue, 7, 8, 18–19, 81
  Barbecue Sauce, 37, 119
  Central Texas–Style Smoked Brisket,
    24, *25*, 26
  From-Scratch Kielbasa, *28*, 29–30
  Ribs, 32, *33*
  Smoked Pork Shoulder, *34*, 35
  Smoked Sausage, 27
  Smoked Turkey, 31
Barley Swine, 147–48, 227
Basic Braised Pork for Tacos, 51, 81
beans, 228
  refried, 76, 157, *166*, 167
  Rice and Beans, 76
  Traditional Pinto Beans, *36*, 38, *39*,
    42, 157
beef, 157. *See also* brisket
  Beef Tongue Empanadas, 174–75
  Bob Armstrong Dip, 70, *71*, 72
  Carne Asada Tacos, 52, *53*
  Chicken Fried Steak with Cream
    Gravy, 99
  Chile con Carne Enchiladas and
    Sauce, *78*, 79, 229

Meatloaf, 118–19
Mustard and Brown Sugar–Crusted
  Ribeye, *103*, 104–5
Old-School Carne Molida Tacos,
  54, 55–56
Beet Fries, *126*, 127
bell peppers, 100, *101*, 231
blackening seasoning, 12
  Blackened Drum with Shrimp Cream
    Sauce, 114–15
  Homemade Blackening Spice, 115
Blonder, Greg, 30
Bob Armstrong Dip, 70, *71*, 72
Bootsie's Buttermilk Pie, 200–201
Braised Pig Tail Puffy Tacos, 49–50
Braised Pork Belly, *60*, 61–62
breads and baked goods, 19
  Cheddar Biscuits, 198, *199*
  Everything Bagel Kolache, *202*, 203–5
  Neapolitan Pizza Dough, 134, *135*,
    136
  Pumpkin Bread, 197
  Texas Citrus Scones, *212*, 213
breakfast and brunch
  Beef Tongue Empanadas, 174–75
  custom tacos for, 156–57
  Gingerbread Pancakes, 172, *173*
  Huevos Rancheros, *166*, 167
  Migas, 168
  Potato and Sausage Breakfast
    Tacos, *158*, 159
  Pumpkin Bread French Toast, 171
  Texas Benedict, 169–70
  24 Hash, 160, *161*
brisket, 19, *28*, 29–30
  Brisket Frito Pie, 38, *39*
  Central Texas–Style Smoked Brisket,
    24, *25*, 26
Bristol-Joseph, Tavel, 213
Broken Spoke, *98*, 99
brown sugar, *103*, 104–5
Buckingham, Jaynie, 206
Bufalina, 124, 134, 136, 159, 226
butter, 105, *208*, 209–10
buttermilk, 108, *109*, 110
  Bootsie's Buttermilk Pie, 200–201
Butternut and Goat Cheese Chile
  Relleno, 81, *90*, 91–92

C

cabbage, *36*, 40
Cactus Jack Cocktail, 189
The Cadillac Bar Pie, 128–29
Carne Asada Tacos, 52, *53*
carrots
  Pickled Daikon and Carrots, *60*, 61
  Central Texas–Style Smoked Brisket,
    24, *25*, 26
chard, Swiss, 81, *90*, 91–92
chayote, 12
  Chayote Slaw with Chile Arbol
    Dressing, 84–85
Cheddar Biscuits, 198, *199*
cheese, 78, 79, 128
  American, 12, 70, *71*, 72, 157
  cheddar, 111, 157, 198, *199*
  cheddar, sharp, *36*, 41, 77, 100,
    101
  Cotija, 58, *59*
  cream, *202*, 203–5
  goat, *90*, 91–92
  Gruyère, 111
  Oaxacan, 13, 88–89
  processed, 12, 72, 73, 77
chicken, 138–39, 157
  Chicken Tinga, 57, 81
  Lucy's Fried Chicken, 108, *109*, 110
  Mole Rojo with Chicken, 81, 86–87
Chicken Fried Steak with Cream Gravy,
  99
Chile Arbol Dressing, 84–85
Chile con Carne Enchiladas, *78*, 79
Chile con Carne Sauce, *78*, 79, 229
chile relleno, 68
  Butternut and Goat Cheese Chile
    Relleno, 81, *90*, 91–92
chiles, 13, 77, 157. *See also* green
  chiles
  arbol, 84–85, 222
  Fresno, 84
  guajillo, 86–87
  Indian long, 144, *145*, 146
  New Mexico, 94, 218, *219*
  roasting, 94, *95*
  sweet red, 227–28
  Thai, 125, 138–39, 147, 227

chilis, 216, 228
    Vegan Lentil Chili, 218, *219*
chipotles, 13, 37
    Chipotle Lamb Loin Chops, 82, *83*
    Chipotle Slaw, *36*, 40
chocolate
    Mexican, 86–87
    Salted Brown Butter and Dark
        Chocolate Pecan Cookies, *208*,
        209–10
chorizo, 13, 157
    Chorizo Potato Pizza, 134, *135*, 136
cinnamon, 86–87, 188
Cirkiel, Shawn, 111
Clark's, 102, 106, 107
Cochinita Pibil, 93
cocktails and margaritas, 178, 184
    Cactus Jack Cocktail, 189
    Colorado Bulldog, 9, 10, 188
    Cucurbit, 186, *187*
    Frozen Margaritas, *182*, 183
    Joanne Cocktail, *190*, 191
    Mexican Martini, 180, *181*
    Mezcal Old Fashioned, 189
Cole, Tyson, 124
Colorado Bulldog, 9, 10, 188
Contigo, 120, 186
Corn Nuts, *150*, 151, 153
cream, 88–89, *103*, 106
    Cream Gravy, 99
    Shrimp Cream Sauce, 114–15
cream cheese, *202*, 203–5
crema, 13, 81, *90*, 91–92
Crispy Masa Shells, 50
Cruz, Nicole, 186
cucumber, 186, *187*
Cucurbit, 186, *187*
Curra's Grill, 93
Cutie Pie Wagon, 206

D

Dai Due, 15, 63, 64
Daikon and Carrots, Pickled, *60*, 61
Daniel Vaughn's Banana Pudding, 211
desserts, 19, 196
    Bootsie's Buttermilk Pie, 200–201
    Daniel Vaughn's Banana Pudding, 211
    Pecan Pie, 206, *207*
    Salted Brown Butter and Dark
        Chocolate Pecan Cookies, *208*,
        209–10
dill, *36*, 43
Dilley, Steven, 134
drinks, 19, 178. *See also* cocktails and
    margaritas

Horchata, 188
    Wundershowzen Smoothie, *192*, 193
Drum with Shrimp Cream Sauce,
    Blackened, 114–15
Duck Confit with Lemon Vinaigrette
    Frisée and Duck Fat–Roasted
        Potatoes, 132–33
Duplechan, Todd, 124, 141

E

East Austin, 132, 162, *163*, 164, 165
Eastside Cafe, 200
East Side King, 124, 127
eggs, 88–89, 157
    Huevos Rancheros, *166*, 167
    Migas, 168
    Texas Benedict, 169–70
    24 Hash, 160, *161*
El Alma Cafe, 222
El Naranjo, 86–87
Emmer & Rye, 124, 143, 213
enchiladas, 47, 231
    Chile con Carne Enchiladas, *78*, 79
    custom, 80–81
    Enchiladas Tejanas, 88–89
equipment, 20–21, 23, 105
Escabeche, 152
Estrada, Regina, 162, *163*, 164, 165
Everything Bagel Kolache, *202*, 203–5

F

fig preserves, 128
Fink, Kevin, 143
Fonda San Miguel, 11, 68, 82, 86, 185
food trucks, 7, 8, 61, 124, 127, 128,
    156, 159, 218, 223
Frank, 169, 198
Franklin, Aaron, 30
Franklin Barbecue, 18
Freedmen's, 18
Fritos corn chips, 38, *39*
From-Scratch Kielbasa, *28*, 29–30
Frozen Margaritas, *182*, 183

G

Garlic, Whole Roasted, *103*, 105
Gilliland, Tom, 68
Gilmore, Bryce, 88, 124, 147, 151
Gilmore, Jack, 88
Gingerbread Pancakes, 172, *173*
Goat Burger, Bakra, 144, *145*, 146
Goldwyn, Meathead, 30
grapefruit, 14

Grapefruit Salsa, 49, 225
Grapefruit Vodka, *190*, 191
green chiles
    Green Chile Mayo, 152
    Green Chile Queso, 77, 81, 157
The Green Sauce, 224
Griffiths, Jesse, 15, 63, 64
Grilled Quail with Green Mole, *140*,
    141, 142
Grilled Tuscan Kale, *103*, 107
guacamole, 70, *71*, *74*, 75

H

Hambleton, Ed ("Edie Eclat"), 218
Hangartner, Emmy, 209
Horchata, 188
hot guts sausage, 19
Hot Sauce, 147–48, *149*, 227–28
Huevos Rancheros, *166*, 167
Hunt, Zane and Brandon, 128–29

I

Indian Long Chile Aioli, 144, *145*, 146

J

Jack Allen's Kitchen, 57, 88, 189, 221
Jacoby's Meat and Mercantile, 118
JAK's Salsa, 88–89, *220*, 221
jalapeños, 144, *145*, 146, 157, 184,
    223. *See also* chipotles
    Jalapeño Cheese Grits, *36*, 41
    Jalapeño Dill Potato Salad, *36*, 43
    Jalapeño Hollandaise, 169–70
    pickled, 38, *39*, 43, 222, 226
jicama, 84–85
Joanne Cocktail, *190*, 191
Joe's Bakery, 73, 162, *163*, 164–65,
    165, *166*, 167, 231
JuiceLand, *192*, 193
Juniper, 124, 130
Justine's, 113, *113*, 132

K

Kale, Grilled Tuscan, *103*, 107
Kennedy, Diana, 68
Kerbey Lane, 8, 171, 197
Kerlin, Bill, 20, 23, 35, 43
Kerlin BBQ, 18, 35, 43
Kirkpatrick, Lance, 21, 22, 23, 26, 32
kolache, 11, 196
    Everything Bagel Kolache, *202*, 203–5
Kome, 124, 137

L

La Barbecue, 18, 31, 40
La Condesa, 84–85, 124
Lamberts, 102, 104
Lamb Loin Chops, Chipotle, 82, *83*
Lenoir, 124, 141–42, 209
lentils
    Vegan Lentil Chili, 218, *219*
Leonard, Jonathan Norton, 228
lime juice, *74*, 75, 85, 138–39, 217.
    See also cocktails and margaritas
Lucy's Fried Chicken (recipe and
    restaurant), 108, *109*, 110, 112, *113*

M

Mackay, Jordan, 30
Magnolia Cafe, 8, 112, 172
Mañana, 203
mango, 137
margaritas. *See* cocktails and
    margaritas
masa, 14, 174–75
    Crispy Masa Shells, 50
Matt's El Rancho, 8, 68, 70, 73, 184
Maudie's, 8, 73, 79, 229
mayonnaise, *126*, 127
    Green Chile Mayo, 152
    Indian Long Chile Aioli, 144, *145*, 146
    Sriracha Mayo, *60*, 61
McGuire, Larry, 102, 106
meat. *See also specific types*
    rubs, 82, *83*
    smoking, 20–23
Meatloaf, 118–19
Mexican Martini, 180, *181*
mezcal, 7, 15, 68–69
    Mezcal Old Fashioned, 189
Micklethwait Craft Meats, 18, 27,
    29–30, 41
Migas, 168
Millian-Torres, Christina, 168
Mi Madres, 156, 168
mint, 85, *190*, 191
Mole Rojo with Chicken, 81, 86–87
Mongers Market + Kitchen, 117
Moorman, Tom, 102, 106
mushrooms, 58, *59*, 81, 138–39, 157
Mustard and Brown Sugar–Crusted
    Ribeye, *103*, 104–5

N

nachos, *150*, 151–53
Neapolitan Pizza Dough, 134, *135*, 136

neon signs, 112–13, *113*
Noble Sandwich Co., 100

O

Odd Duck, 11, 124, 151, 191
Okra with Walnuts, 120, *121*
Old-School Carne Molida Tacos, *54*,
    55–56
orange juice, 63, 93, 180
orange liqueur, 180, *181*, *182*, 183,
    184, 185
oranges, 63, *212*, 213
Oxtail Pappardelle with Rutabaga,
    130–31
Oysters, Baked, *116*, 117

P

Palm Dressing, 84–85
pancetta, 143
pantry staples, 12–15
The Peached Tortilla, 46, 61
peanut butter, *192*, 193
pecans, 14, 86–87
    Pecan Pie, 206, *207*
    Salted Brown Butter and Dark
    Chocolate Pecan Cookies, *208*,
    209–10
pepitas, 15, *140*, 141, 142
peppers. *See also* chiles
    bell, 100, *101*, 231
    poblano, 58, *59*, 77, 94, 152, 157
    roasting, 94, *95*
Pickled Daikon and Carrots, *60*, 61
Pickled Jalapeños, 38, *39*, 43, 222,
    226
Pico de Gallo, 217
Pig Skin Noodles with Shrimp
    Dumplings and Hot Sauce, 147–48,
    149
Pimento Cheese, 100, *101*
Pistachio Cream Sauce, 90, *91*–92
pizza
    The Cadillac Bar Pie, 128–29
    Chorizo Potato Pizza, 134, *135*, 136
pomegranate, 90, *91*–92
Pommes Puree, *103*, 106
poppy seeds, *202*, 203–5
pork, 15, 143, 157. *See also* bacon;
chorizo; sausage; wild boar
    Banh Mi Tacos, *60*, 61–62
    Basic Braised Pork for Tacos, 51, 81
    Braised Pig Tail Puffy Tacos, 49–50
    Braised Pork Belly, *60*, 61–62
    Cochinita Pibil, 93

Pig Skin Noodles with Shrimp
    Dumplings and Hot Sauce,
    147–48, *149*
Ribs, 32, *33*
Smoked Pork Shoulder, *34*, 35
Texas Benedict, 169–70
potatoes, 157
    Chorizo Potato Pizza, 134, *135*, 136
    Duck Fat–Roasted Potatoes, 132–33
    Jalapeño Dill Potato Salad, *36*, 43
    Pommes Puree, *103*, 106
    Potato and Sausage Breakfast Tacos,
    158, 159
24 Hash, 160, *161*
prickly pears, 15, 189
pumpkin puree
    Pumpkin Bread, 197
    Pumpkin Bread French Toast, 171
pumpkin seeds. *See* pepitas

Q

Quail with Green Mole, Grilled, *140*,
    141, 142
Quality Seafood, 114, *115*
queso
    Bob Armstrong Dip, 70, *71*, 72
    Green Chile Queso, 77, 81, 157
Qui, Paul, 124

R

radish, *60*, 61, *150*, 151
Ranchero Sauce, *166*, 167, 231
Ravago, Miguel, 68
ribs, 19, 32, *33*
rice, 157, 188
    Rice and Beans, 76
    Sunshine Roll, 137
Rockman, Amanda, 196, 203
rutabaga
    Oxtail Pappardelle with Rutabaga,
    130–31

S

salsa, 216, 224
    Grapefruit Salsa, 49, 225
    JAK's Salsa, 88–89, *220*, 221
    Pico de Gallo, 217
    Salsa de la Casa, 222
    Salsa Macha Verde, 223
Salt and Time, 174
Salted Brown Butter and Dark
    Chocolate Pecan Cookies, *208*,
    209–10

salts, 13, 29–30, 186, *208*, 209–10
sauces and dressings, 81. *See also*
    mayonnaise; salsa
    Barbecue Sauce, 37, 119
    Chile Arbol Dressing, 84–85
    Chile con Carne Sauce, *78, 79*, 229
    Cream Gravy, 99
    Green Mole, 81, *140, 141*, 142
    The Green Sauce, 224
    Hot Sauce, 147–48, *149*, 227–28
    Indian Long Chile Aioli, 144, *145*,
        146
    Jalapeño Hollandaise, 169–70
    Lemon Vinaigrette Frisée, 132–33
    Mole Rojo, 81, 86–87
    Oxtail Ragu, 130–31
    Palm Dressing, 84–85
    Pistachio Cream Sauce, *90*, 91–92
    Ranchero Sauce, 81, *166*, 167, 231
    Shrimp Cream Sauce, 114–15
    Verde Sauce, 81, 230
Sauerkraut Johnnycakes, 143
sausage, 19, 157
    From-Scratch Kielbasa, *28*, 29–30
    Potato and Sausage Breakfast Tacos,
        158, 159
    Smoked Sausage, 27
seafood, 15, 102. *See also* shrimp
    Baked Oysters, *116*, 117
    Blackened Drum with Shrimp Cream
        Sauce, 114–15
    Sunshine Roll, 137
    Uchiviche, 125
Second Bar + Kitchen, 75
sesame seeds, 86–87, *140, 141*, 142,
    202, 203–5
shrimp
    Pig Skin Noodles with Shrimp
        Dumplings and Hot Sauce,
        147–48, *149*
    Shrimp Cream Sauce, 114–15
sides, 19, 36
    Barbecue Sauce, 37, 119
    Beet Fries, *126*, 127
    Bob Armstrong Dip, 70, *71*, 72
    Brisket Frito Pie, 38, *39*
    Chayote Slaw with Chile Arbol
        Dressing, 84–85
    Chipotle Slaw, *36*, 40
    Green Chile Queso, 77, 81
    Grilled Tuscan Kale, *103*, 107
    Guacamole, 70, *71*, 74, 75
    Jalapeño Cheese Grits, *36*, 41
    Jalapeño Dill Potato Salad, *36*, 43
    Pimento Cheese, 100, *101*
    Pommes Puree, *103*, 106

Rice and Beans, 76
    Traditional Pinto Beans, *36*, 38, *39*,
        42, 157
Silverstein, Eric, 61
Smoked Pork Shoulder, *34*, 35
Smoked Sausage, 27
Smoked Turkey, 31
smoking meats, 20–23
spinach, 157, *192, 193*
squash, *90*, 91–92
Sriracha Mayo, *60*, 61
steakhouses and dinners, 98, 99, 102,
    103, 104–5
Stiles Switch BBQ & Brew, 18, 21, 22,
    26, 32, 42
Sunshine Roll, 137
Sway, 124, 138–39
Sweet Potato Nachos, *150*, 151–53
Sweet Red Chile Ferment, 227–28
Swift's Attic, 11, 49, 225

T

Tacodeli, 52, 188
tacos, 46, 47, *47*, 223
    Banh Mi Tacos, *60*, 61–62
    Basic Braised Pork for Tacos, 51, 81
    Braised Pig Tail Puffy Tacos, 49–50
    Carne Asada Tacos, 52, *53*
    Chicken Tinga, 57, 81
    custom breakfast, 156–57
    Old-School Carne Molida Tacos, *54*,
        55–56
    Potato and Sausage Breakfast Tacos,
        158, 159
    Tacos de Hongos, 58, *59*, 81
    Wild Boar Carnitas, 63, 81
Tamale House East, 46, 55
tequila, 15, 178, 189. *See also*
    cocktails and margaritas
Texas Benedict, 169–70
Texas Chili Queens, 218
Texas Citrus Scones, *212*, 213
Tex-Mex and interior Mexican, 9–10,
    68–69, 73. *See also specific recipes*
tomatillos, *220*, 221, 230
tomatoes, 120, *121*, 157, 218, *219*.
    See also salsa
Tom Kha Gai, 138–39
Torrealba, Ernesto, 86
tortillas, 15, 47, *47*, 48, 50, 168. *See
    also* tacos
Traditional Pinto Beans, *36*, 38, *39*,
    42, 157
Turkey, Smoked, 31
24 Hash, 160, *161*

U

Uchi, 124, 125
Uchiviche, 125

V

Valera, Carmen, 55
Vasquez, Moses "Baby Moe," 55
Vaughn, Daniel, 21, 23, 24, 30, 211
Vazquez, Reyna and Maritza, 159
Vega, Iliana de la, 86
Vegan Lentil Chili, 218, *219*
Veracruz All-Natural, 134, 156, 159,
    223
Verde Sauce, 81, 230
Via 313, 124, 128–29
Voyles, Evan, 112–13

W

walnuts, 120, *121*
Walsh, Robb, 30, 73
Whip-In, 124, 144, 146
Whisler's, 189
Whole-Grain Mustard Butter, 105
Whole Roasted Garlic, *103*, 105
wild boar, 15, 64–65, *65*
    Wild Boar Carnitas, 63, 81
Wiseheart, Andrew, 120
Wundershowzen Smoothie, *192, 193*

Y

Yanes, Nicholas, 124, 130

Restaurants Pictured

Broken Spoke, *98*
Cafe Mañana, *196*
Dai Due, *10* (second from right), *65*
Fonda San Miguel, *48*
Joe's Bakery, *163*
Justines, *113*
La Condesa, *10* (second to left),
Micklethwait Craft Meats, *10* (left), *27*
Lamberts, *10* (right),
Lucy's, *113*
Quality Seafood, *115*
Stiles Switch BBQ & Brew, *2*
Whisler's, *179*
Veracruz All Natural, *3*

Editor: Holly Dolce
Designer: Heesang Lee
Production Manager: Rebecca Westall

Library of Congress Control Number: 2017945117

ISBN: 978-1-4197-2893-8
eISBN: 978-1-68335-222-8

Printed and bound in China
10 9 8 7 6 5 4 3 2 1

Abrams books are available at special discounts when purchased
in quantity for premiums and promotions as well as fundraising or
educational use. Special editions can also be created to specification. For
details, contact specialsales@abramsbooks.com or the address below.

ABRAMS The Art of Books
195 Broadway, New York, NY 10007
abramsbooks.com